After the
B☐XES
are
UNPACKED

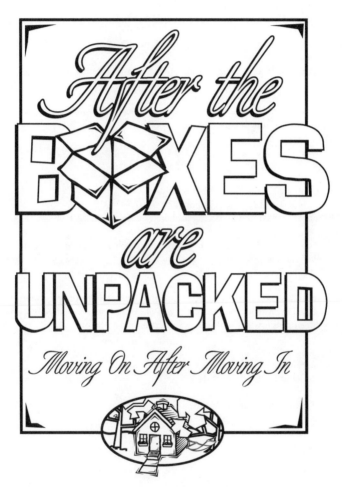

After the B⬦XES are UNPACKED

Moving On After Moving In

Susan Miller

Tyndale House Publishers, Wheaton, Illinois

Library of Congress Cataloging-in-Publication Data
Miller, Susan
    After the boxes are unpacked: moving on after moving in/Susan Miller.
       p. cm.
    ISBN 1-56179-405-8
    1. Women—Religious life. 2. Moving, Household—Religious aspects—
Christianity I. Title.
BV4527.M54 1995
248.8'43—dc20   95-9344
                                                 CIP

A Focus on the Family Book Published by
Tyndale House Publishers, Wheaton, Illinois 60189
Renewing the Heart is a registered trademark of Focus on the Family.

Editor: Gwen Ellis
Designer: Bradley Lind
Cover Illustration: Bradley Lind

Printed in the United States of America

    01/10 9 8

To Bill
I'd follow you to the ends of the earth.

After the Boxes Are Unpacked is like a visit from a new neighbor! Susan's warmth, creativity, and encouragement are akin to a Welcome Wagon drawn up to your front door. This book is a comfort, a resource, and a heart-talk, all wrapped up together. How wonderful to be able to give this book to neighbors, friends, relatives, and newcomers to our church.

Daisy Hepburn
Director of Women's Ministries
Scottsdale Bible Church

The inward struggle of the heart to adjust to a new plan, a new calling, and a new community is very real. Susan Miller has done a superb job in offering biblical insight and practical ways of addressing the loneliness, trauma, needs, and challenge for women who have moved to let go emotionally and move on to a new location. You cannot read this book without being challenged to personally evaluate the people and things you cherish most.

After the Boxes Are Unpacked would make a great gift for a new pastor's wife who has moved to your community, for newcomers who attend your church for the first time after a job transfer, for a friend or relative who is moving to "unknown territory," or as a gift of hospitality and outreach to a new neighbor.

Jean Milliken
Northwest Women's Ministries President
Conservative Baptist Church

Relocating can be a frightening exprience as women leave friends and families and attempt to adjust to a new area—sometimes to cultural differences. In a delightful way, Susan Miller gives us in *After the Boxes Are Unpacked,* practical handles on how to address this need of our times.

Martha Baker
Director Women's Ministries
Fellowship Bible Church
Little Rock, Arkansas

Contents

Part III MOVE AHEAD

Foreword

For many couples, their major goal in moving is to stay married. For singles, the need is to maintain their sanity—and to find that "special friend" with a truck! As someone who has packed way too many haul-it-yourself trucks in his time, I know that moving can rank right up there on the "fun things to experience" list with wallpapering, root canals, pet-sitting a pit bull, and having your 12-month-old triplets all start to teethe at the same time.

Let's face it: Moving may never be fun. But now comes a resource that can take a great deal of the pain out of having to pack, the smarting out of having to uproot the kids, and the sting out of leaving family and friends. Far better than any welcoming service are the insightful experiences, biblical advice, and clear-headed counsel that Susan Miller offers in this book. This is vital information that can help you before the boxes are packed and then guide you through the many adjustments still being made months after everything is on the shelf.

Believe me, Susan's been there. She and Bill, her husband, have moved more than a dozen times. She knows the financial, emotional, and spiritual challenges that come with a change of address. She knows what it's like to leave parents and best friends, search for a new church, hunt down a seemingly nonexistent reasonable rental home, and find a doctor in a strange city at midnight. More than that, she knows how to grow spiritually during those times of incredible transition, as well as where to find the courage to put down roots all over again.

Not only has Susan lived out the principles you'll learn in this powerful, hands-on resource, but she has also taught them to hundreds of people just like you. Susan's Newcomers Enfolding and Welcoming (NEW) ministry has been a wonderful success at the home church we share, Scottsdale Bible Church. Now her program is being picked up by wise churches across the country, and I think it should be a required ministry in every church that's serious about welcoming newcomers.

I know you'll be blessed by what Susan has to say in this book. And there's also another reason her book is such a blessing to me. Susan's words represent the first book in the new *Encouraging Words* imprint line that I'm honored to be launching with Focus on the Family Publishing.

For years, I've had the privilege of informally coming alongside a number of authors and helping them develop a book. When Focus on the Family approached me about working more formally with authors from within a book line, I was intrigued. They spoke of a line that would carry the same name as my ministry—*Encouraging Words*—and I prayed long and hard about what such a thing would look like. Certainly, any authors whose books carried my ministry name must share three traits.

First, I'd only work with people I knew personally and believed in wholeheartedly.

Second, they had to be people who had a long-term track record of serving and loving the Lord and could clearly articulate that love to others.

And third, they had to be able to put practical, biblical help within easy arm's reach of those experiencing a heartfelt need.

Susan Miller fits all those criteria. It's an honor for me to help introduce her to you as a wonderfully talented author, and to launch an *Encouraging Words* book line with her words of hope to those facing or already dealing with transition.

In addition, I want to thank Dr. James Dobson, Al Janssen, Gwen Ellis, and the rest of the Focus on the Family Publishing team for starting this new book line.

My prayer is that this book and each one that follows will build your faith and strengthen your family.

God's best to you,

John Trent, Ph.D.
President, *Encouraging Words*
Phoenix, Arizona
August 1995

Acknowledgments

From the movie, *Enchanted April*, I vividly recall the line, "No one should ever write a book that God wouldn't like to read." I kept that in mind as I wrote this book. First and foremost, my goal was to honor and glorify God through my writing. I know that without God's faithfulness and guidance, this book could not have been written. To Him, I am most grateful.

Many people accompanied me on the journey of writing this book. Without them I could not have made it to the finish line. My heartfelt thanks to the following people:

John Trent, you encouraged me from the beginning of the Newcomer's Ministry at SBC to write this book, opened the door for me to do it, and then held my hand through the process. Thank you for all you've done to make my dream a reality. You never gave up on this book and you never gave up on me.

Gwen Ellis, my gifted editor. I remember so well the afternoon we met to get acquainted and go over my first chapter. Your words of encouragement that day, and what you taught me about writing, gave me the confidence to proceed. Thank you for believing in me as a writer. Your inspiring influence was key in writing this book.

Al Janssen, director of book publishing at Focus. You caught my vision and enthusiasm over dinner one evening. Thank you for believing in the need for this book.

Larry Weeden, the first at Focus who encouraged me in my writing. I was so excited to visit with you for my first "book talk." I remember I slid down the bannister for joy.

Jerry West, who, when it comes to computers, is a genius! Thank you for your teaching, coaching, and endless long-distance calls from Atlanta to walk me through "what to do next" and "which button to push!"

Nancy West, my beloved friend for over 20 years. You were the catalyst for this book when I moved from Atlanta. You taught me that friendship will not only last, but will deepen and grow, regardless of distance. I love you dearly!

My team of readers, the "Steadfast Six"—*Sudie Althisar, Nancy Del Duca, Mary Malouf, Bob Malouf, Jackie Oesch* and *Sandy Richmond*. All of you spent hours reading and critiquing my manuscript, correcting the grammar and spelling (and my famous run-on sentences!), and giving valuable feedback that would more clearly communicate the message of God's hope to women who move. Each one of you also share a special link to this book.

Nancy, without whom I could not have finished this book. You believed in me when I didn't believe in myself. Chapter by chapter, day and night, you listened and encouraged. I cherish you!

Sandy and Sudie, you teamed with me to start the Newcomer's Ministry at SBC. Our lives will never be the same. You are as much a part of this book as I am.

Jackie, you gave me the first opportunity to expand my ministry to newcomers beyond my own church and across the nation. God used you as part of His plan to make it happen. I am so grateful for you.

Bob and Mary, your biblical and spiritual wisdom kept me centered within the pages of the book and keeps me centered in the pages of my life.

The *"31 Calendar Girls!"* dear friends who committed to a day of the month to pray for and uphold me during the months of writing. Your expressions of love and support carried me from day to day!

Karen Erickson, you were that still, small voice in my ear that gave me the push I needed.

Donna Otto, you paved the way as an author and a friend.

Darlene Danninger, you keep the vision alive at SBC.

All my *"Moving Friends"* who shared their stories, their insights, their joys, and their struggles in the moving process. You have given life to the pages.

Bill and Ginger, you are the joy of my life. If we hadn't moved, you would have never found Ann and James! My prayer is that this book will minister to each of you as your journey in life with your mate is just beginning.

And most of all, to my husband *BILL*, who has been the love of my life for 30 years. No one person was more instrumental in my finishing this book than you were. Thank you for believing in me, for encouraging me, for listening to me, for critiquing page after page, for gourmet coffee and cookies that would appear by the computer, for taking care of me and for loving me so dearly. I've always said you were the wind beneath my wings. Now I know why. You have enabled me to soar to heights I never dreamed of through writing this book.

Introduction

What You Need to Know

What happens when you move? It's so important to have an understanding of what you are going through and to know that you are not alone. Any woman who moves goes through a grieving process. She experiences a tangible loss. It's often devastating for a woman to relocate. And if she is single and relocates, the experience is even more traumatic since she has no backup support system.

Some of the most difficult hurdles in moving are leaving behind friends and family, losing familiar surroundings, and feeling a great sense of spiritual loss. Women go through not only the stages of loss, but also of disbelief, grief, and anger before they recover. I have even labeled this trauma as a "closet illness" because so many women have said to me, "I didn't know anyone else felt like this." "I thought something was wrong with me because I was so angry and bitter at my husband for this move." "I felt as if I was the only one going through this kind of adjustment."

There are millions of women, like yourself, experiencing the effects of trauma and transition that moving brings. According to the Bureau of the Census, U.S. Department of Commerce, *Geographical Mobility*: March 1991 to March 1992, the number of women 20 and over who move each year is 15 million! Of that total, over 5 million women move to another county or state. From March 1991 to March 1992, over 42 million men, women, and children moved! That means one in five people or 20 percent of the population move each year.

Research has long since shown that moving is one of the top 10 traumas. No wonder you feel the way you do! In the pages that follow, there is hope and encouragement to get you through the major impact of a move. I've worked with hundreds of women just like you, and equipped them with the tools for a smoother transition. In each chapter I'll be giving you principles to move by and I'll walk with you through the process. I'll share with you what I've learned through my own experiences in moving, along with the wisdom I've gained from teaching and counseling women who have faced what you are facing. Throughout the book, I'll draw from a reservoir of my "moving friends" who have so lovingly shared their suggestions and stories in order to help women like you through the transition of moving.

You can make it!

From my heart,

Susan Miller

PART I

Let Go

Chapter 1

From Grits to Guacamole

For though I am far away from you, my heart is with you.
Colossians 2:5, LB

It was four o'clock in the morning, and just beginning to rain as we walked down the driveway to our van. Bill, Bill Jr., Ginger, and I were setting out on another journey into the unknown. Our beloved friends, Nancy and Jerry, had let us spend the night with them, since we had left our house empty and clean for the new owners. We fought back tears as we realized our lives would never again be so intertwined with Nancy and Jerry's. As we exchanged hugs and kisses good-bye at the end of the driveway, the pain of loss and separation became real. The rain began pouring down, and we rushed into the van, not lingering to form the words that stuck in our throats. Silently we asked ourselves the question, *When will we see each other again?*

Once in the van, I rolled down the window to Nancy. Our faces almost touching, our eyes brimming with tears, I whispered, "I just don't know if I can make it one more time!"

Nancy answered encouragingly, "Yes, you can, and you will with God's help. Now go!" I quickly rolled up the window, and as we pulled away, I held back tears of sorrow. I reassured Bill and the children that I was going to be okay. I knew in my heart that somehow I had to find it in myself, once again, to let go of all that was near and dear, and to start over, moving ahead with a new life.

As we began our long journey westward, I reflected on all of our previous moves. Some had been good—a chance for a new beginning, a fresh start. Some had been a part of Bill's climb up the ladder of success. Some had been easy and others hard—especially as our children got older.

Moving is more than loading and unloading boxes. It's leaving behind everything familiar to face the unknown. There are countless questions: How am I going to find new doctors and dentists? Where are the grocery stores and which one is best? When is garbage pickup day? Who will be my new television weatherman? On what radio station will I find good listening music?

Finding answers even to simple questions can cause grief to someone who is moving. And the big ones are overwhelming even to think about. How do I find a new church home? What about making new friends? Oh, the effort and energy it takes!

How could I start over when I hadn't even begun to let go of my old life? I felt the loneliness of being so far away from family and friends creep in. I felt the almost unbearable fear of leaving behind an ill mother. I felt anger and bitterness as I asked, *Why do we have to move again? Why do we have to move so far away from all that I am, and all that I identify with?* I fought back the familiar depression and the dread of the unknown that crowded my mind.

My mind switched back to the present. The bags really were packed and the van really was loaded down with valuables that couldn't be shipped ahead. The rest of life was in brown boxes in a moving van headed for a destination 2,000 miles away. Once again I was pulling up stakes. Once again I was saying good-bye to friends. At this moment, I didn't belong anywhere; not in the old city and not in the new one down the road. The emptiness overwhelmed me.

I smiled for the children's sake, to give them a sense of security that everything was going to be all right. I engaged in some "meaningful" conversation with Bill, to assure him I was indeed standing by his side in this transfer and was united with him in this move.

The sun began to rise and the rain stopped. The air was fresh and the day felt new in the early morning dawn. With the breaking of day came peace, the hope of new opportunities and new challenges. A smile came not just to my face but to my heart, and I felt God by my side. He was the Friend who would go with me. He would ease my hurt and bring me contentment. God would never leave me. I knew He was already at my destination, waiting with open arms.

A reassuring scripture came to mind, "The Lord Himself goes before you and will be with you; He will never leave or forsake you. Do not be afraid; do not be discouraged" (Deut. 31:8, NIV). I leaned over, kissed Bill on the cheek, and broke the silence by exclaiming, "Isn't this a beautiful day to start a new journey together!" I took a deep breath, and in the quietness of my heart, said to myself, *I am going to make it one more time, Lord!*

Westward Ho!

It seems like only yesterday that we moved from Atlanta to Phoenix. We were making our 13th move in 18 years of marriage. With Bill in the hotel business, moving was a reocurring part of our life together.

In this particular move, we looked like the Beverly Hillbillies with our loaded van, two children, one dog, six pieces of luggage strapped on the top, and a U-Haul trailer in tow carrying all my plants! (We always try to hold onto everything and take it all with us, don't we?) Of course, I didn't realize that after a three-day journey in that U-Haul, with no air and all that heat, when I opened the door I'd find all my plants dead!

All our previous moves had been within the Southern states, and being a Southerner from South Carolina, I had never been 2,000 miles away from my roots. We had never ventured past the Mason-Dixon line, and what I knew of the West was only that I'd be eating guacamole instead of grits.

I soon learned I would be surrounded by cactus instead of oak trees, that "desert landscaping" would be a new term in my vocabulary, and pronouncing Spanish with a Southern accent would always get a laugh!

Part of me anticipated the opportunities a new place would offer, and part of me was sad to leave behind our family, our church, established friendships, and our Southern roots. Still another part of me was just plain weary. I wanted to be like the tiny doodlebug that hides by burying itself in the sand. The thought of moving to a new place and starting all over again was both challenging and depressing.

Sometimes it's hard to see God in the midst of our circumstances, as it was when we ventured West. I'm thankful He's always there, whether we see Him or not. The Lord has been a stronghold in my life for 13 moves, and I realized that together, He and I could do it one more time.

We arrived in Phoenix in August, the hottest month of the year. I cried the entire month. I couldn't get used to seeing all those rocks in yards, some which were even painted green to look like grass! *And where was everybody?* How was I to know they had all left Phoenix to get out of the 120-degree heat!

Bill and I had come to Phoenix in July for a weekend house-hunting trip. Those three-day decision-making trips never allow enough time to learn the area in which you want to live. There's never enough time to find the best schools and a house you can afford that will hold all your furniture. Needless to say, we didn't find anything on that trip; so when Bill went on ahead of us to start work, he bought a house which I had never seen before arriving in Phoenix. Until we closed on the house, we lived in a hotel for two weeks. Of course, you know what that's like—the glamour wears off quickly!

The first thing I did was to make the children's transition as smooth as possible. Bill, Jr. was going into the ninth grade and Ginger into the sixth grade. I knew it was crucial that they get settled in quickly, so I registered them not only in school but on a soccer team, since they both had played in Atlanta. They started practice even before we moved into our house.

All the things I had to do raced through my mind! I knew I needed to get everything squared away by myself because Bill would be preoccupied with his new job.

I also remembered how moving always created a loss of identity and affected my self-esteem. Once again I thought, *If I don't give too much of myself away, it won't hurt as much when we leave the next time.*

Bill *was* preoccupied with his new job and started traveling immediately. I spent the days trying to learn which streets would take me where I wanted to go and get back to the place from where I started. I used the time while we were still in the hotel to make all the necessary arrangements for the house—telephone, utilities, and mail service.

With Bill and the children settled into a routine, it was time to tackle the house itself. The empty rooms chilled me, despite the 120-degree heat. The big moving van containing the bulk of our furnishings arrived and the movers dumped the furniture and boxes carelessly in each room. I was left to take each pile of stuff and once again make this house a home for us. Slowly, as I unpacked each box, hung the pictures, placed accessories and cherished momentos, and added a few new plants, I began to feel comforted by all that was familiar.

By the time the house was settled, school had started. Bill was entrenched in his work, and I set out to find my niche in Scottsdale, the area of Phoenix where we had settled.

I soon learned Scottsdale was referred to as "La La Land," the home of the rich and the famous! I certainly didn't feel like a "La La Lady!" It seemed everyone played tennis and golf, or jogged in cute little outfits with cute little bodies to match! I was already emotionally fragile from the move, overly sensitive to the spider veins in my legs, painfully conscious of my "thunder thighs," and totally aware of the extra 20 pounds I'm always trying to lose. My self-image was pretty low. I didn't seem to measure up. I struggled with living in a world where my Southern heritage didn't fit. I was terribly homesick and missed the close relationships of family and friends.

I knew that coming to Scottsdale was part of God's plan for our family. Yet I knew there were plenty of changes that needed to take place in me, before I could even begin to call this place home. When our family moves, finding a church is very important. It is a vital way for us to establish our roots. We visited many churches before we found Scottsdale Bible Church. It was here that our life as a couple and as a family was enriched and we began to grow. Here Jesus Christ became the *center* of our lives, not just a part.

In my 20s, I had rededicated my life to Christ. In my 30s, we were baptized together as a family, and in my 40s it was as if God said, "Go West and grow! 'For I know the plans that I have for you'" (Jer. 29:11).

As my security in Christ deepened, my self-image began to change. I only desired to measure up to God's standards, not the ideals of those around me. Gradually, my feelings of inadequacy diminished. I still have spider veins and thunder thighs, and I'm still 20 pounds overweight—but on a sunny day you'll find me in shorts! I tried tennis lessons, but I could never get the ball and the racket to make a connection; it's too hot to play golf; and I prefer to walk instead of jog!

It's hard to believe we've been in Scottsdale 14 years now, the longest time we've ever lived in one house. Recently, I found myself actually having to clean closets—a task that frequent moves had always made unnecessary!

"Do not call to mind the former things, or ponder things of the past. Behold, I will do something new, now it will spring forth; Will you not be aware of it? I will even make a roadway in the wilderness, rivers in the desert" (Isa. 43:18-19). And indeed He has!

Maybe you are where I was—grieving over leaving family and friends, concerned about your children's adjustment, confused about knowing which doctor to call, wondering where to find a good church. It can be overwhelming! But in 13 moves, I've learned some biblical principles that have not only helped me get by, but have taken me ahead spiritually. I'll be sharing those principles with you in this book, along with the steps I had to go through to adjust to moving.

A Journey of Healing

Looking back, I can clearly see and understand the three-step process of healing and adjustment that helped me through the trauma of moving. If it helped me, it can help you as well. Let me share those steps with you.

I. Let go
II. Start over
III. Move ahead

Let go. The first step in my process of healing was to choose to *let go* and leave behind any encumbrances that would prevent me from starting over and moving ahead. I had to allow God to *mend* any feelings and emotions that kept me from being the whole, happy, and productive woman He wanted me to be. I had to choose to be *open* to God's love. So many times when we had moved, my spirit had been closed because of the anger, bitterness, depression, loneliness, stress, expectations, comparisons, or separation anxiety (just to name a few) that I felt. Until I learned to understand my feelings, and go through the process of letting go, I couldn't be open to receiving God's love and healing. I couldn't really begin the process of starting over. This time, I knew there was plenty of mending that needed to take place in my life, and I was prepared to let God start stitching!

Start over. I also had to choose to *start over*. I had to be open to allowing God to *mold* me through this process. As part of starting over, I needed to work through the feelings of loneliness, loss of identity, and inadequacy which threatened to overcome me at times. On the home front, I had to build our nest all over again, recognizing the effects that moving had on the children, and remembering to keep my marriage ties strong. Of course, I had to be ready for the challenges and opportunities that new beginnings bring to each of us! Until I allowed God to refine me and teach me through the process of starting over, I couldn't be ready to move ahead with my life.

Move ahead. Finally, I had to choose to *move ahead.* Notice I always use the word "choose." I believe it is my choice to either be open or closed to change and to what God is teaching me. I realized it was time to take my eyes off myself and to start thinking of others. It was time to come full circle by feeling God's contentment. I needed to move in the right direction, with God as my focus. I couldn't mature in Christ until I allowed Him to mend and mold me. I couldn't move ahead with my life until I was willing to let go and start over. As I persevered in my walk with Christ, I felt the fulfillment and joy that only He can bring into our lives!

My process was to:

> let go
> start over
> move ahead

God's process was to:

> mend
> mold
> mature

The journey of healing is one of action, according to God's plan. I let go—God mends me. I start over—God molds me. I move ahead—God matures me.

Take My Hand

Enough about me. I want to talk to you—the newcomer, the wounded traveler. This book is written for you, my friend. I have walked in your shoes, felt your joy in the good moves and your pain in the bad ones. God has put you on my heart. He has taken me down the road of 13 moves to be able to turn around and reach out to you, taking your hand in mine.

Perhaps you've just moved. Maybe you're getting ready to move. Maybe you're dreading it and maybe you're looking forward to it. My prayer is that this book will help you through the process of letting go, starting over, and moving ahead with your life, seeing God in the process.

I will take you through the process step by step. We'll laugh together; we'll cry together; but most of all, we'll grow together. Remember, you are not alone! Take my hand, and I'll tell you the rest of the story as we walk the journey together.

"Now to Him who is able to do exceeding abundantly beyond all that we ask or think, according to the power that works within us, to Him be the glory!" (Eph. 3:20-21)

Chapter 2

Leaving Behind

Like a shepherd's tent my dwelling is pulled up and removed from me.
Isaiah 38:12

I feel so detached," Mary Jane was telling me how her move was affecting her. "My entire root system is gone! I feel like a plant that has been pulled from fertile soil, then left to shrivel up and die. This feeling of rootlessness is overwhelming me. I just want to be put back in that pot, packed with soil, and fertilized!" she said with her eyes full of emotion. Mary Jane had left behind her mom, dad, two sisters and their families, a small business she owned, and an abundance of friends. This was her first move and she was devastated.

What Mary Jane left behind had an enormous effect on her ability to adjust and start over in her new location. When I met her she had just arrived in Phoenix and, as she put it, she "just couldn't get a grip." She even looked like a withered flower. Her shoulders drooped, she looked pale, and when I hugged her, her body was limp. It was obvious this young woman needed lots of hugs and someone who understood her loss. Mary Jane was grieving all she had left behind.

When I explained what was happening to her, she said, "You mean what I feel is normal? I'm really not weird or crazy?" I assured her she was not weird or crazy and that she was going through a grieving process much like that which happens when a death or divorce occurs.

Here are the steps of grieving that movers experience:

Denial. Mary Jane refused to accept that Phoenix was her new home. She made no attempt to make new friends, or do the obvious things that claim residency, such as getting an Arizona driver's license or Arizona plates for the car.

Anger. Deep down she was angry with her husband and blamed him for taking her away from her family, friends, and successful business.

Depression and sadness. Reality had set in, which was why Mary Jane fit the description of a withered flower. She realized this move was for real, and she wasn't going to get to go home tomorrow.

Acceptance. Mary Jane could not start putting her roots down until she accepted her circumstances. She needed to be willing to leave the past behind to start over for the future.

In her book *Women and Their Emotions*, Miriam Neff explains, "Grief is experienced when we must adapt to separation from any person who is important to us, or to an extreme change that has been a meaningful part of our life." [1]

Neff says that grief is a process rather than a series of stages. How true this is in the case of moving! No one can set a time frame for how long it will take to go through the process of grieving and adjusting. We all respond differently—we all walk to the beat of our own drum. For some women it takes weeks, for some months, for some even years. Sadly enough, some never make the transition.

Neff also points out that it's not time itself that is the healer, but rather what happens during that time. I have seen women successfully start over by making every effort to make it happen, and I've seen women literally become stuck in their own grief and misery. How much significance you place on what you left behind, and how you have faced change in the past will play a big part in how well you adjust and adapt.

I wanted to help Mary Jane get a grip, and also to help her understand what she was going through. With my arms around her, I said, "Mary Jane, it's all right to cry. Everything and everyone you left behind is worth every tear. Your tears are a part of your healing right now, and you must not keep them bottled up inside." And cry she did. It was as if she needed permission to let the flood gates down. It was a healthy release for her.

When the tears subsided, I went on. "Mary Jane, I want you to remember you are not alone here. You may feel cut off from your family and your friends, but you are not cut off from God. He didn't bring you here to abandon you."

Just hearing those words seemed to give her new assurance, and we spent the rest of the afternoon helping her to put her life in perspective. I wanted her to know that even though God can do great things in our moving process, there would be emotional lows that are a normal part of letting go. Mary Jane began to understand that the feelings of numbness, emptiness, and sadness were all a part of the loss she felt. I went over again the vital things she needed to remember:

- You are not weird or crazy
- You will go through a grieving process
- It's okay to cry
- You are not alone

It was important for Mary Jane to know that God has much to say to those of us who pull up stakes and move. I shared with her some of my favorite moving verses:

"For I know the plans that I have for you . . . to give you a future and a hope" (Jer. 29:11).

"The Lord Himself goes before you and will be with you; He will never leave nor forsake you. Do not be afraid; do not be discouraged" (Deut. 31:8, NIV).

I also gave her the verse that had been most dear to my heart during our move to Phoenix, and I give it to you to claim as your moving verse:

"Do not call to mind the former things, or ponder things of the past. Behold, I will do something new. Now it will spring forth; will you not be aware of it? I will even make a roadway in the wilderness, rivers in the desert" (Isa. 43:18-19).

This verse says to me, "Don't dwell in the past. God will do something new here and eventually it will be obvious to you. He will make a way for you in this unknown place and bring the cool refreshing waters of a new life to your barren heart." What a reminder that God is in charge, and that He will bring about new things! With our Lord, there is hope for the future!

♥   Heart Talk   ♥

Can we heart-talk for a minute? That's when I just talk heart-to-heart and down-to-earth with you. Remember this, because throughout this book we're going to have a lot of heart talk!

When we moved from Decatur, Georgia, to Raleigh, North Carolina, I left behind my dream house. It was a time in our lives when we were still chasing rainbows. We were excited about Bill's promotion and what it would mean to his career. But I didn't want to leave, for I had found at the end of my rainbow a house that I loved, and that I felt loved me back, and it was in Decatur. That house and I seemed to be in perfect harmony. The more of myself I put into the house and yard, the more joy and contentment it seemed to give me in return.

It was a three-level house built on the side of a hill, with a brook flowing through the backyard. The living room had a 16-foot ceiling with glass windows from top to bottom overlooking the woods. What memories I have of that place!

The hotel Bill was managing at the time had a 12-foot palm tree they were going to get rid of because it looked so puny. Ahhhh, the perfect accessory for a house with a 16-foot ceiling! I gave it a new home, named it Percy the Palm Tree, and nursed it back to health. Our dear friends Nancy and Jerry were even married in that house, under the palm tree.

As we drove away from Decatur, all I could see in the rearview mirror was that wonderful house. It had become my security and my identity. It was the place where I belonged. I didn't care about finding another house in Raleigh. I knew nothing else would ever come as close to being me.

We looked and looked for the "right" house in Raleigh—in the "right" school district, the "right" neighborhood, and for the "right" price! We found all the "rights" by building our house. I had the opportunity to pick out colors, carpet, and tile to make the new house as close to being me as possible. It helped. No, I couldn't fit a 12-foot palm tree into the living room and, no, it wasn't as large as the one I'd left behind. But, it had a great deck that overlooked the woods!

I learned a lot about myself and about houses from that move. In fact, God has taught me something important through every move, every house, and every place we've lived. Have you ever stopped to ask yourself, "What is God trying to teach me through all of this?" I learned that:

- My security does not come from a house (or any other thing, for that matter). Real security comes only from trusting in God.
- A house can only bring you happiness; it can't make you happy.
- You never grow if you always stay in your comfort zone. Spiritual maturity comes in learning to depend on God to meet your needs.
- Things should not be held too tightly. They can keep you from embracing what God has planned for you.

When you look in the rearview mirror, what do you see? In the process of letting go, you must first deal with what's back there, because what you left behind will affect you. As you look back, you probably see your family, those dear friends, a house you loved, a church where you worshiped, and a city you called home.

In Audrey McCollum's book *The Trauma of Moving*, she says, "Leaving behind a broken rocking chair in which the first-born was soothed to sleep, a piano around which there was caroling at Christmas, a rusty tricycle—whatever embodies special memories and experiences—can feel like an amputation. It is the loss of a segment of family continuity, of personal history, the loss of a fragment of self." [2]

As women, we have an overwhelming need for a sense of belonging, a sense of community. That feeling of attachment to someone or something is often lost in the transition of a move. The pain of separation and the feeling of rootlessness often leave us feeling wounded, affecting our ability to start over.

Never Say Never!

"Do what, Abraham? Go where? How far is it? How long will it take?" his wife, Sarah, asked in complete shock. She had never thought about moving! Abraham was successful in his home city of Ur. They had a nice home and financial security. Then one day, Abraham came home and said, "Sarah, God has told me to leave here and move to another country. I don't know where we're going. I only know He's commanded this and I must obey," (See Genesis 12–23.)

Can you imagine the questions and feelings that went through Sarah's mind? "But . . . but Abraham, what about our home? What about our friends? I don't know if I can leave this place where I've lived since I was a child. We've been in this home since we were married. I grew up here, and now you want to take me away to a strange land, with no idea of where we're going, or how we're going to get there!"

I can only begin to imagine the clutched feeling in her heart. I can see her having a tent sale and selling everything that couldn't fit in a pack to be carried by a camel. I envision her giving her fine silk garments to friends, and cherished heirlooms to family members. She likely gave flowers and vegetables from her garden to her neighbors. Their family and friends probably gave them a farewell party. I'm sure there were laughter and tears and lots of hugs; and then Sarah and Abraham were gone, swallowed up in a cloud of dust from their caravan. Sarah left behind much that had been her security.

I can almost feel Sarah's heart wrenching as she left her beloved home for an unknown place. She went with Abraham out of love, commitment, and obedience; but I know she must have been torn emotionally between staying and leaving, as many of us have been at some time. Like all of us, I'm sure Sarah, too, learned a lot about herself from that move. She discovered that her security came from trusting God for what lay ahead, not in what she left behind. She found that God moved her from her place of comfort to a place of spiritual growth. She learned not to hold onto things too tightly in order to embrace what God had planned for her.

Sarah and I and many other women who have moved have learned, "Never say never!" In His time, God showed both Sarah and me His plan. Sarah gave birth to a child she thought she would never have, and I got to move back to Georgia!

Learn from Those Who Have Gone Before You

I always like to share Abraham and Sarah's story with women who have moved or are moving. Not only can we identify with Sarah, but by observing Abraham, we can learn valuable lessons that will equip us for any journey. The Lord said to Abraham, "Go forth from your country, and from your relatives, and from your father's house, to the land which I will show you" (Gen. 12:1). "And he went out, not knowing where he was going" (Heb. 11:8).

Abraham responded to God's command, and he learned from the experience. God takes those who move on a journey of:

Obedience. Abraham didn't *react* to going; he *responded* to going! He didn't react by getting upset, arguing, and being negative. His response was to obey and just do it! Abraham sought to do God's will, not his own will. It's so difficult when the transfer comes, or the new job means relocating, to always respond with a positive attitude and with enthusiasm when you really don't want to go. But it is a choice we make—a choice to rebel or obey, to walk *with* God or walk *away* from God.

Faith. Abraham's faith was in the promises of God and in knowing that God would fulfill His covenant. It takes a lot of faith to face the unknown. But what a comfort it is to know that God promises not to leave us or forsake us! (Deut. 31:8) My faith is wrapped around God's promises in scripture. I've traveled down many roads reciting my favorite scripture verses and holding on to nothing more than God's promises.

Trust for provision. Abraham knew God would cover all the details if he would simply trust Him. When our house in Georgia didn't sell, I had to trust that God was in control. When nothing went according to plan, I had to trust that God had everything figured out. I had to have faith that God was working through all the details of all of my moves. It's in that moment of complete surrender and trust, when you truly let go and let God take over, that your life takes on a new direction.

Hope for the future. Abraham had great hope for tomorrow and for God's plan to be fulfilled. With each move, my heart held new hope—hope for our future, our dreams, our plans. That hope became part of my persevering spirit. I know it's hard to leave everything behind and move to a place that is unknown. But, never lose hope in what God is capable of doing through this transition in your life.

These principles from the lives of Sarah and Abraham are basic; when they are applied to your own life, they will equip you for any journey you will ever encounter.

Survival Kit

Mary Jane, my moving friend you met at the beginning of this chapter, asked me for some practical suggestions to help her adjust to her new life and situation. This is what I gave her—a survival kit.

Things that will make your transition easier:

- Plan on having a high phone bill for a time after you move. Get a good long-distance calling company and the maximum calling plan.
- Don't always call. Try to write letters to family or friends back home.

This process will help you realize you are separated by many miles. And writing helps you clarify and communicate your feelings.

- Make a "home tour" video to send to family and friends. Include the house, yard, kids, dog, new neighborhood, the kids' new friends, schools, church, and everything else a video camera can record.
- Take a family group picture holding a sign that reads, "We love you," or "Remember us," or whatever message you want to send. Make lots of copies and send them to friends.
- For fun, clip "job opportunities" from the classified section of the paper and send them to your friends with a note that says, "Come join us!"
- Plant flowers, bulbs, and seeds to remind yourself that you, too, are putting down roots to grow here.
- Keep a journal. Putting your thoughts and feelings on paper will be healing for you. Months from now, it will be good to look back and see where you were and the progress you've made toward settling in.
- Subscribe to a magazine or local newspaper from back home to help you bridge the gap. I still get *Southern Living* to keep myself connected!

Do you *cherish* or do you *cling to* what was left behind? Let's move on to the next chapter and find the answer.

Chapter 3

Cherish, Not Cling

Though time and miles may separate us,
I have built a bridge of lovely memories to span the distance.
Virginia Tubbs

I cherish the card that my friend Betty from Atlanta sent me with that verse printed on it. I kept it in my keepsake box for 14 years, along with other special cards and notes I received other times we've moved. I even had it framed and kept it on my kitchen counter the first few years we were here in Phoenix, as a reminder of all the precious memories, family, and friends we left behind in Georgia, Florida, and South Carolina.

I have a black and white picture of Betty, Nancy, and me—we called ourselves The Three Musketeers! It was taken in the '70s and there we are, posing with our look-alike hairdos parted down the middle. It sits on my desk along with other pictures of the three of us taken over the years. The pictures and the framed verse are reminders of how long we've been friends. Neither time nor miles has diminished our devotion and love for each other. I have cherished those two women as friends and sisters in Christ for over 20 years; yet for 15 of those years we've been separated. We are proof that a cherished friendship never dies.

I also left behind Marian and Dee, who were mentors to both Bill and me; and I left behind Cindy, who was first our children's teacher, and then became a dear family friend. Marian and Dee still mentor Bill and me through their love and devotion; and Cindy has continued to influence our children long after they are grown. I cherish all of their friendships, and yet we live 2,000 miles apart.

Furthermore, I left behind my immediate family—Mama, Daddy, and my brother, Bob, and his wife, Peggy, when we left Fort Walton Beach, Florida. I cherish the imprint they've made on my life. An artist draws a subject on canvas to give it substance and form, then paints it to give color and life. Daddy gave me the substance and form and Mama gave me color and a love for life. I see Daddy living on in my brother, Bob, and Peggy has been the best sister-in-law to me and daughter-in-law to Mama that any family could ever have.

I cherish the memories of our family gatherings around the dining room table. Mama celebrated every occasion, every holiday, and always had theme decorations for the table! I treasure the view of the Destin Bridge with its shades of blue water from the Gulf of Mexico gleaming underneath. I fondly remember the wild sea oats that grew nestled in the sand dunes on the "world's most beautiful beaches."

I value my South Carolina heritage—magnolias, oak trees, barbeques, family reunions, the "low-country," hammocks, front porches, and fried chicken. All these remembrances are like buds, ready to blossom at any moment into a bouquet of lovely memories. I cherish what I've left behind. It permeates my life with a fragrance that is identified with who I am.

To Cherish . . . To Cling

I have often looked back and thought, *What if I had chosen to cling to the past rather than cherish it? What if I had chosen not to let go? Could I have ever really started over in all our moves?*

Dianna lived in Arizona for 29 years before moving to Minnesota. I spent time with her before she left, trying to prepare her for the road ahead. She later wrote to me from Minnesota and said, "I'm not very good at letting go. I kept remembering that you said I needed to, but I kept resisting.

Holding on, though, keeps me from benefiting from the new blessings God has for me. Thanking God for things in my new place gets my mind going in the right direction. And another thing that helps, ironically enough, is going home. It helps me let go. When I go to my old home, it makes me realize that I have a new one. It takes away the mystique. Sort of the way getting back together with an old boyfriend reminds you of the problems that had somehow disappeared as time went by."

♥   Heart Talk   ♥

Let me share a little insight with you as we heart-talk. The more I thought about cherishing and clinging, the more I asked myself the question: *What should we cherish, and what should we cling to?* I'm a visual person and it helps when someone shows me, simply and clearly, the differences between two ideas. Perhaps you've never really thought about what a difference understanding these two words will make when you adjust to a new home.

To cherish means "to hold in the mind, to treasure, to hold dear, to value highly." To cling means "to clutch, to cleave, to hold on to, to grab hold of." Lets apply those definitions to moving.

- *Cherish what was!*
- *Cling to what is and to what never changes!*
- *Cherish what you left behind!*
- *Cling to what you brought with you!*

The following are examples:

Cherish	Cling to
Distant Family	God
Distant Friends	The Bible
Past Memories	Your Faith
Your Heritage	Prayer
The Job You Left	God's Promises
The House You Loved	Positive Not Negative
Your Roots	Your Values
The Place (City/Town) You Left	Each Other

What are you holding onto that is keeping you from moving forward? You owe it to yourself, your husband, and your children to begin the process of letting go. You must discern between what to cherish and what to cling to! I'm not saying any of this is easy. It reminds me of times when I'm in the ocean, trying to swim with the waves to shore, only to find that the undercurrent pulls me back out again. It's a constant struggle trying to go forward and then being pulled back into the sea. The only time I make it to shore without being swept back is when I stand up and walk forward. Sometimes the only way we can stop from being washed back into a sea of memories and can make it to our destination is to stand firm, walk forward, and not allow anything to pull us back. The force of the current is still there, but we choose to move away from its undertow.

A Contented Penguin

Allicia has moved 10 times. Her last move was from California to Florida. She shared with me how hard it was for her to connect with others after so many moves. "I hesitated to connect at first because leaving friends is like having a favorite pet that gets run over—you just hate to replace it because you know perhaps the new one could get run over, too." She went on to say, "I noticed a pattern in my moving. The places that were the most meaningful to me were the ones where I needed God the most. They were also the ones where I prayed the most. The more intimate I was with God, the more time I spent with Him, the more I grew. I began to put my expectations not in a place, but in a Person. Because my places have changed and will again, I must fasten my heart on something else, for where my treasure is, that's where you'll find my heart. My heart must be stabilized in God, who is unchanging."

I love what she said next: "On my refrigerator is a verse from Philippians 4:11, 'I have learned to be content in whatever circumstances (state) I am.' Below that is a picture of a penguin on a tropical island under an umbrella, sitting on a large icecube sipping tea, with the words: 'For I have learned in whatever *state* I am, to be content!' Contentment is the result of much prayer. It produces a peace within me and then within my husband and my children."

Allicia is an example of a woman who has learned to *cling* to God and to prayer in her moves.

Across the Miles

Cherish the past, recognizing that God will single out relationships that will endure, no matter the time between visits and the miles between you. Lasting friends are like cream that rises to the top. Your acquaintances may be many, but cherished friends will rise up to stay in your heart forever. Here are some things that can be done for family and friends to deepen and enrich relationships across the miles:

Remember birthdays. Remember, it's the thought that counts! Mailing a gift can get expensive, so be creative and try my "birthday-party-in-a-card" idea! I keep balloons, confetti, birthday banners (they come in a crepe paper roll—just tear a few "Happy Birthdays" off), streamers, napkins, and other birthday supplies on hand. A balloon, some confetti, two birthday banners, a few streamers, and a napkin will all fit neatly into an envelope. I write on the card, "Since I can't be there, I'm sending a party-in-a-card!"

There are some other small remembrances that will fit in a card—bookmarks, hankies, teabags, a packet of seeds, a pressed flower—to name a few. Don't forget books and stationary; tapes are great to mail, and they fit right inside a mailing envelope.

Remember Christmas. Send newsletters, magazine subscriptions (we sent *Arizona Highways* to our family so they could learn about the state), framed pictures, an ornament characteristic of your locale. (I mailed little ceramic cacti one year, also plastic chili peppers, a tin cowboy boot—sounds hokey but they'll look cute on your friend's tree!) Don't forget other special occasions, too.

Plan your phone calls for Saturdays and Sundays, when rates are lowest. Don't forget the time change! Many times we've called and awakened family and friends at one or two in the morning!

Make a prayer calendar with names of friends, family, and children on each day of the month. Put their state or city underneath the name. Don't forget to include yourself! Make copies and send to everyone. What a great reminder to pray on a certain day of the month for a special person and to know others are praying for you!

Plan visits so you'll always have something to look forward to! It's comforting to know there is a certain time set aside and a commitment made for a visit. Our friends would always plan to visit us in April when the desert is in bloom, and we would go home for the 4th of July for family reunions and beach time.

Be creative in ways that span the miles. The first year we were in Phoenix, I wanted to send Nancy something that would remind her we would always be connected. I went to a holiday boutique and met a lady who personalized needlepoint. I had her make "The Arizona-Georgia Connection" and then had it framed. It still sits on Nancy's bookshelf as a visual reminder of our special friendship.

Try some of these suggestions. They will ease your transition and and help you to cherish those you left behind.

The Flying Trapeze

Until you let go of the past (release it) and begin to cherish it (hold in mind, treasure, hold dear), you can't cling to (cleave, hold on to, grab hold of) the present, and embrace the future.

A friend recommended Paul Tournier's book *A Place for You*, during my preparation for this book. He gives a wonderful illustration of letting go that I have shared with many women and want to pass on to you:

> I thought of the trapeze artists, swinging on their trapezes high up under the dome of the circus tent. They let go of one trapeze just at the right moment, to hover for a moment in the void before catching hold of the other trapeze. As you watch, you identify yourself with them and experience the anxiety of the middle of the way, when they have let go of their first support and have not yet seized the second. . . . What is the force that holds men back, which prevents them from letting go of what they would like to let go? It is the middle-of-the-way anxiety. It is the void in which they are going to find themselves before being able to seize a new support.
>
> All this to say, we must always be letting go . . . leaving one place in order to find another, abandoning one support in order to reach the next, turning our backs on the past in order to thrust wholeheartedly toward the future.[1]

When I read Tournier, it brought back vivid memories of going to the circus as a child. I remember the times when two trapeze artists would catch on to the same bar and, with hands clasped together, would swing toward the other trapeze. Then they'd release the one they were holding and almost instantly catch the new one. They always worked in twos or threes, swinging together, hand in hand. Sometimes one person waited at the new bar, ready to reach out and grasp the hands of the trapeze artist, while another stayed behind to help push off.

But underneath there was always a safety net! If someone fell, he or she quickly bounced back up and kept on going. Do you see what I see? God is the One who clasps your hand as you move from one place to another. He is the One who has gone ahead of you, prepared a place for you, and will hold out His hand for you to cling to. He was with you when you started, and will be with you when you finish. If you should fall along the way, He will be there to protect and guide you, and make sure you keep going! Thank You, God, for this blessed assurance to all who move!

Walk in Their Shoes

Once again I am reminded of ordinary people who did extraordinary things through their journey with God.

Noah. It's one thing to travel over land, but over water? He didn't even think about getting seasick! Noah trusted God and showed great courage in his journey. God did not forget him nor forsake him (Gen. 6–9).

Abraham. God told him to go to an unknown land (Gen. 12–25). He was to just pick up and go, no questions asked. He went in faith and obedience. I would have dug my heels into the sand!

Moses. God took him out of his comfort zone to face adversity through Pharaoh, his enemy. God let him wander in the desert for 40 years (Exodus–Deuteronomy). What a trip that was!

Paul. During his journey to the city of Damascus, he came to know Christ and became one of the greatest missionaries of all time (Acts 13).

No matter where you've been, where you are, or where you are going, knowing Jesus Christ can change the course of your life. For these people, their journey, or move, provided an opportunity to establish a deeper walk with God. They had unlimited opportunity to trust Him, to depend on Him, and to cling to Him. What opportunity does your move provide?

Marian, a moving friend who lives in Colorado, says it so well, "Realize that God places us where we are, to prepare us for what He wants us to become." Never forget, the road has been traveled before you. The choice to cherish the past and cling to God for the future is not always easy, but faith, hope, perseverance, prayer, and obedience are the keys.

"I do not regard myself as having laid hold of it yet; but one thing I do: forgetting what lies behind and reaching forward to what lies ahead, I press on toward the goal for the prize of the upward call of God in Christ Jesus" (Phil. 3: 13-14).

Survival Kit

Here are some ways to help you cherish the past and cling to the future:

- Don't expect things to be the same in your new location as they were in the old one, or you'll be disappointed.
- Focus on what you have here, not on what you had there.
- Accept being where you are.
- Send samples of your new culture to family (seashells, fruit, rose petals—whatever is typical of your new area).
- Send "a piece of who you are" to friends (favorite book, recipe, poem, verse—whatever you love).
- Let go of expectations that you'll move back.
- Dwell on the positive and not the negative.
- Write your family or friends and tell them how much you cherish them in your life. Written words are keepsakes!
- Find a new church. When you have found one, you are home.

In the next chapter, we are going to talk about some important initials, MAD, and their big impact on your move!

Chapter 4

What Moving Affective Disorder Does to You

Be strong and courageous! Do not tremble or be dismayed,
for the Lord your God is with you wherever you go.
Joshua 1:9

"I'm going to explode!" Ann said, as she raised her voice above those of the other women in the room. You could have heard a pin drop as silence fell over the room and all eyes turned to Ann. About 20 newcomers were gathered for a weekly newcomer's class at our church.

"I feel like someone lit my fuse six months ago when Jim told me we were going to move; we've been here for one month now, and my fuse is getting shorter and shorter!"

Her voice was beginning to break with emotion, and you could feel the empathy rise in the room. Some of the women had been there; others were at that moment feeling the same turbulence within themselves. "What's happening to me?" Her eyes pleaded as she spoke, "I feel like I'm going to jump out of my skin! My life has been turned upside down, I'm exhausted, and there are still boxes that haven't been unpacked. I can't find things I need in the house, not to mention the grocery store. I yell at the kids for no reason, and my husband is too busy to help me hang the curtains."

Someone laughed and broke the ice by saying, "Welcome to the MAD world of newcomers! You've got what we refer to as Moving Affective Disorder! It comes from the stress overload factors that moving creates."

Ann smiled slightly and questioned, "What in the world is that, and is there a cure?"

I spoke up and said, "Oh, yes! There's a cure all right. Time is a big influence, but there are lots of other things that can help you too. First of all, though, let me explain what we mean by Moving Affective Disorder.

"Since there are labels and names for everything that comes down the pike these days, it just seemed natural that we should have our own term for what we go through when we move. No one really seems to believe that the trauma and transition of moving is serious. It's like a closet illness. The stress that movers go through has been hidden away for too long! Yet it affects every area of our lives, often leaving us devastated. Our lives are like a puzzle that's been turned upside down, and we have to somehow put all the pieces back together in order. We thought it would be healthy for all women who go through the same thing when they move, to have a name they can temporarily hang their hat on! It breaks the ice and makes us laugh!"

MAD was a new insight for Ann, and helpful for all of us who are willing to acknowledge the stress that is unique to us as movers.

The Overload Factors in Moving

As we continued to talk, I said, "Ann, let me tell you what the stress overload factors in moving are. I think it will help you understand this feeling that you're going to explode."

I explained to her that anything that exceeds our normal stress level can throw us into overload very quickly. (We all have a stress level that varies, depending on the circumstances of our lives.) People are like washing machines: We get out of balance when we have too many clothes piled in on one side. Overloaded washing machines make terrible noises and threaten to tear everything apart! So, to avoid that, we have to stop the washing machine, redistribute the clothes or take some out, then start it again.

It is the same way with us. When we get out of balance or tilted, we have to stop, balance our load or eliminate part of it, and start again. From the moment we find out we are going to move, whether we're happy or sad about it, our stress level will rise. The anticipation, preparation, and expectation, all rolled into one, takes us off the routine path of life and sets us up for stress. Our minds start anticipating the changes to come. Our to-do list becomes overwhelming. All this happens before we even begin moving! We still don't know what to expect when we get to our destination.

Most of us have people who will help with the physical move, but few of us have anyone to help with the emotional move. Even under the best circumstances, emotional stress is inevitable. Moving puts us on the overload cycle!

Several years ago, I went to a seminar for newcomers sponsored by the Phoenix Parks and Recreation Department. Because of the number of new people moving to the Valley of the Sun, as our area is known, the park department offers a one-hour information session on how to adjust to the area and to the heat. I have shared some of the information from that seminar with the Newcomer's Class I founded at church, and with other movers I've met as I've traveled across the nation. I'm so thankful to our park and recreation department for meeting this particular need. (Perhaps you can recommend this idea to the park department where you live. It's a great way to meet new people.)

The information I got from them indicates that stress overload factors fall into these three categories:

Packing and unpacking. It's stressful to pack and unpack our lives, for during the process, we relive the memories attached to our possessions. Then the physical labor leaves us exhausted. And when something is broken or damaged in the move, it is one more loss.

Adjustment to new location. There are so many little things that can add up quickly and throw us off balance. Just finding answers to these questions is stressful: When is mail delivered? When is garbage pickup? Where's the best grocery store, bank, dry cleaner, doctor, service person, mechanic?

Destructive comparisons. We compare everything: the weather was better back home, the traffic wasn't as bad, the people were friendlier. We tend to remember the good about where we used to live more than the bad. *Everything* appears better than it truly was. It usually takes about a year to balance out the comparisons.

Stress can show up in a physical manner. Know your own body and watch for weight gain or loss, backaches, headaches, and other physical symptoms. It can also show up in emotional highs and lows. Watch for them and seek help before they become severe.

You're in Good Company

To help you put this whole thing in perspective, there are over 42 million people, 15 million of whom are women, who move each year. [1] You're in good company. We share a common bond with all those women! We've all suffered in some way or another from MAD!

After Ann exploded at our newcomer's class, several of the women chimed in to tell her their own moving stories and experiences. It was a comfort to Ann. Here are their stories:

"I expected moving to be an adventure, to be lonely and hard, to add hassle and stress to my life, yet to be culturally enriching, to draw us closer as a family, to be a challenge to our marriage, to stretch me spiritually. I was looking forward to the relief of not working and to just being a mom. I knew it would be painful to have my kids grow up far away from my parents. At the same time, I thought it would be exciting to be surrounded by all this history. Moving was all of that," Dianna boldly stated. She had moved twice in less than two years. Then she added, "By the time all the preparations are done, I'm ready to leave. I get tired of saying good-bye. I reach a point where I just want to get it over with. I get nervous, scared, and excited. Then it's such a weird feeling to get off a plane in a new city and think, *I just moved here. This is my new home. I live here now.* It seems like it should take longer and be more difficult than a plane ride."

Dianna went on, "At first, Ann, it's so exciting! I love to buy new things for the house, try out new restaurants, check out the malls, and discover all the new places to go. Then, when all that wears off, it stops being exciting and becomes frustrating. It takes time to adjust and accept all the changes."

Beverly, who has moved nine times, spoke up in a gentle voice, "Realize it will take time to adjust. Things won't be the same, but even though they're different, they may be better. God is faithful. He won't leave us. And we do grow from each new experience."

Sudie, who has moved 10 times, said calmly, "Believe it or not, a major stress for me was trying to find the right hairdresser! That's so important to all of us. I'd travel across town for the right haircut. My hair is an expression of who I am, and as it is, I already lose enough of my identity when we move."

Alma, who has moved three times, laughed and said, "The biggest adjustment for me was going from a very busy lifestyle with a full calendar, to a calendar with nothing written on it!"

Judy, who has moved 10 times, spoke from experience, "I allow myself the freedom to feel the pain of moving. It's difficult. Don't expect too much too soon. I have to make positive choices to begin nesting in the new place. If my feelings get too overwhelming, I take a break and go to a movie. Live today; look for the positive; and don't burden everybody with negatives."

God truly does work in wondrous ways through His people to touch the lives of others—through compassion, through sensitivity, and through understanding. When someone has walked in your "movin' shoes," they know the road you've traveled. We all felt good after the women had shared their thoughts and feelings, and offered encouragement to Ann. Our morning had given purpose and significance to one more mover!

The Apache Trail Experience

A life change, like moving, is not always easy; but then, God doesn't always want to make it easy for us, for it's in those stressful times that we grow closer to Him. Sometimes God allows us to go through an experience for the powerful lessons we could learn no other way. I remember a particularly stressful time when we first moved to Phoenix. I ran away from home. To this day, I can't even remember the specific reason; I only remember I felt like a balloon that had been filled beyond capacity and would burst at any moment if the pressure were not released. My release was to leave.

I got into my unreliable compact car early one morning, and proceeded to drive southeast of Phoenix with my eyes fixed on the beautiful Superstition Mountains. They looked like a place of refuge for me, an oasis in the middle of the desert. I rolled the windows down and felt the cool October morning air on my face. I let the wind blow through my hair and I let the tears roll down my cheeks as I turned off the main highway toward the mountains. The sign said "Apache Trail," and I remembered reading something about it being an authentic Indian trail. That sounded adventurous enough, so I kept going. I soon came to a sign that said, "Pavement ends—proceed at your own risk." *Why not?* I thought, feeling daring and unafraid. The road went higher and higher into the mountains. Then it became a switchback trail, getting rougher and narrower; then the Apache Trail became a ledge on the side of the mountain with a tremendous drop to a lake down below. It was impossible to turn around. The only way out was to keep going.

About that time the car began to stall, sputter, and overheat. I kept turning the key in the starter for fear it would completely die out. I knew if it stalled, I'd be stranded with no phone, no passing cars, and no people in sight. I was in the middle of nowhere. Now, I'm not a fearful person, but the reality of what was happening hit me—I had no control over the situation. I was completely alone and had foolishly put myself in a dangerous predicament. The car could have gone over the side of the trail, down the canyon, and into the lake. It could have stalled. If that had happened, I would have been stranded for who knows how long and I would have been at the mercy of anyone who might show up on the trail. I was afraid for my life.

All of a sudden, everything came into perspective. Nothing seemed as important as getting to the other side of the mountain, so I could go home to Bill and the children. I prayed out loud as I clutched the steering wheel. I said my favorite Bible verses over and over. I sang all the hymns I could remember. My perspective changed from focusing on the stress that moving had caused, to focusing on my relationship with God. Not only did I feel His presence in the car, but I actually felt Him in control as the car miraculously kept going.

After two hours on the Apache Trail—two hours of an intense refresher course about who God is in my life—I saw the highway in the distance ahead. It was 80 miles back to Phoenix, and I didn't dare stop the car, knowing it wouldn't start again. It was almost dark by the time I sputtered up the driveway and said, "Thank You, Lord, for getting me home safely. I'll never do that again!"

God taught me some powerful lessons that day. For one thing, I haven't done anything that foolish since! The other things I learned are in our Heart Talk.

♥   Heart Talk   ♥

Whatever trail you might be on emotionally after your move, just remember:

Do not tremble. When the road gets rough, slow down, take a deep breath, put things in perspective, and depend upon God to get you through the circumstances. He *will* enable you to make it.

Do not be dismayed. When you can't turn around, focus on God and on what's in front of you. Looking back isn't going to help you get beyond the move. If your focus is on Him, God will equip you with whatever is necessary to move ahead.

The Lord your God is with you wherever you go. When you feel alone and afraid, remember who accompanies you! Turn to God for the comfort of His presence and the calming of your fears. He will embrace you as a friend with His word. God will protect you—He is behind, alongside, and ahead of you.

Be strong and courageous. When your vehicle (your body and emotions) starts to fail you, realize you're out of control and consciously, verbally, give God the steering wheel in your life! Depend on Him to get you through this crisis. Let His strength be your strength. He will encourage you and uphold you.

Remember, when you are on overload and stressed out from your move, God will . . .

Enable you
>*Equip you*
>>*Embrace you*
>>>*Encourage you*

"Have I not commanded you? Be strong and courageous! Do not tremble or be dismayed, for the Lord your God is with you wherever you go" (Josh. 1:9).

Survival Kit

To help you reduce the stress of moving:

- Don't get too upset over broken things. Something always breaks or gets damaged. Remember, they are just things.
- Pick one room and concentrate on getting it settled so you have a place to rest while everything else is in disarray.
- Trust God . . . even when it seems everything is going wrong.
- Join an aerobics class—a great stress reliever.
- Remember, Rome wasn't built in a day, and your house won't be settled in a day either.
- Pray about everything.
- Have one goal per day. Don't try to get new license plates, a library card, and a driver's license all at once.
- Reward yourself with a special treat such as a new nail polish or a magazine when you accomplish a dreaded task.

- Treat yourself to an old favorite stress reliever—a hot bath!
- Go to a bookstore and browse.
- Read the book you've always wanted to read.
- Listen to "praise tapes," or a good Christian radio station.
- Read the Old Testament book of Exodus. What they accomplished was so much more complicated and difficult than any of our moves. It will help put your move in perspective!
- You can always claim Scarlett O' Hara's famous line, "I'll think about that tomorrow!"

Did your move leave you with a "ding" or a "nick"? How quickly will you recover? Lets find out in the next chapter!

Chapter 5

A Ding or a Nick?

In Him all things hold together.
Colossians 1:17

One Saturday morning as Bill was washing the car, he called me over to look at the door on the passenger side. "What happened here?" he asked, as he pointed to an obvious dent in the door.

"I don't know what happened," I replied. "Surely, I didn't do that!"

"Well," he said, "looks like somebody put a pretty strong ding in the side of your door. That's not going to be as easy to fix as a nick would have been."

"What do you mean, not as easy to fix?" I asked curiously. "What's the difference between a ding and a nick?" (I felt as if I was having one of those bonding conversations with Bill.)

"Well, I'll show you the difference," he said, as we walked to the other side of the car. "This is a nick," he pointed. "It's just a chip and it can be touched up with matching paint. The difference between a ding and a nick is the force of the blow."

"Bill, now it's clear to me!" I said in excitement.

He laughed as he said, "Well, it's not that hard to figure out, Susan!"

"No, no, I mean that's the way it is when you move! A move can be a ding or a nick, depending on the impact. If a move is a ding, then it's going to be harder to adjust than if the move is just a surface nick. The adjustment should be a lot easier in the case of a nick. The impact of a nick can be repaired from the outside. The repair can come from a surface change, like a smile on the face. A ding, however, has to be repaired from the inside. And for the mover with a ding, the change has to come from internal healing, or restoration. It really does depend on the force of the blow."

So I ask you, was your move a ding or a nick?

A Moving Experience

To help you answer that, let me ask you three questions:

Was your move planned or unplanned?

Was your move expected or unexpected?

Was your move wanted or unwanted?

I ask these questions of newcomers a lot, because they give me a quick handle on the movers' situation. Many women and families look forward to moving. It can mean a promotion, a better lifestyle, an opportunity to start over, a chance to live in a different climate, financial and professional advancement, retirement, health reasons, a chance to be near family, or they could just be ready for a change. These people have the opportunity to plan ahead and be prepared. For those who expect a move, there are no surprises. They know it will come, and they live with knowing they are not going to be in their current place for long.

For those who want the move, it can be a happy experience. It can be anticipated with enthusiasm. But even moving for all the right reasons can lead to disillusionment, disappointment, and unmet expectations. That, in turn, can determine whether your transition is a ding or a nick! *How you start the move is important; how you finish the move is also as vital to your own wellbeing as it is to your family's.*

On the other hand, it can make a big difference if the move was unplanned and you had two weeks notice to be at the new location. If it was unexpected and you had no choice in the matter, if it was unwanted, and you had no desire to go, this makes a great difference.

The "Steel Magnolias!"

Women from across the nation have shared their stories about the impact of their moves and how they affected their lives. No one seems to escape the kaleidoscope of emotions that comes with moving. From stay-at-home moms to single career women, from pastors' wives to military wives, from corporate wives to professional sports wives, they all share a common bond when it comes to moving.

Many of them have given me permission to share their stories with you. They hope, in some way, to give you greater understanding and insight into your own move. Some of their moves were "dings" and some were "nicks." Try to identify them yourself.

Debbie's husband is in youth ministry. After living in one place for 11 years they took another position . They left behind both sets of parents and a strong support system of friends. Their move was unplanned and unexpected, yet it was a chance to do something new and expand his ministry. After a year, Debbie still finds it very hard to make friends in their small community where most residents have lived all their lives. She finds it difficult to break into the circles of families and friends already deeply rooted there.

When Dianna moved from New Jersey she said, "I was so glad to leave, that I even forgot to tell my house good-bye!" They had been expecting a transfer. However, they didn't particularly want to go to Minnesota.

Joan's move to Connecticut was not necessarily her first choice, but she was ready for the move, knowing when a promotion came for her husband, he'd leave within two weeks. She can usually get a house sold and herself packed and moved within three to four months. Although she was sad to leave her friends and church, she was happy to reunite with her husband after four months and start to settle their house.

Linda is a single mom. After her divorce, she wanted to start over, so she moved to Arizona with her two children. She was deeply hurt over the divorce, but she knew she had to keep going. Her first priority was to find a job and a place to live. She knew no one and chose Arizona to get as far away from old memories as possible.

Dot is married to a professional athlete. I call her a gypsy mover. She might have to move twice a year if her husband is traded to another team. She lives month to month and year to year, based on her husband's performance in the game. Even though they can afford to buy any house they want, it's still hard to put down roots. When they move, Dot's husband has instant friends on the team, but she often doesn't have a single friend to turn to. She says that even though they live an affluent lifestyle, she feels alone and anxious about being uprooted so often. "I don't always want the next move, but I always have to expect it," she said.

Joanne and her husband had successful careers in a large city. When he became ill and had to retire, they decided to move from the city to the country for a simpler life. "We hadn't planned on moving, nor expected to move at this time in our life—but knew we had to make a major change in our lifestyle."

Pam celebrated her 40th birthday two weeks after they moved back to Texas. She said, "I felt too old to start over again!" It was easier when her children were younger; now they were teenagers and that made it harder. She thought it would be exciting to reunite with old friends and familiar territory, but was soon disappointed that a lot had changed in the three years they'd been gone.

With her husband in the military, moving has become part of life for Tracey and their two-year-old daughter. They've moved twice in their four years of marriage. Tracey looks forward to new opportunities, new culture and new friends. However, as a young mom in a new place, she often feels lonely and isolated. "It's always hard when you're new and don't know anyone who you can spend time with besides the baby, or even know anyone who can baby-sit."

Laurie, a pastor's wife, had settled in their church and had just finished remodeling their home. She was expecting their second baby. Then, her husband was called to pastor another church. "It was very hard to leave a congregation we loved and start building relationships all over again," she said sadly. Laurie struggles with the thought of moving.

Until We Meet Again

"Karen," her nametag read. She was working at the library the day I went there to do some research on this book. I walked up to her desk, told her I was writing a book for women about moving, and asked if she could assist me. "Moving?" Karen said, "I'll tell you about moving!" I sat down in the chair next to her desk and prepared to listen. I could tell by her voice that I had exposed a painful subject and that she wanted to talk about it. "Do you mind if I write this down? I might be able to use your experiences in my book." This is Karen's story:

When Karen's husband was transferred to Kentucky, he had to start work there immediately. She stayed behind in Phoenix to sell the house and wait for the children to finish out the school year. In the meantime, she went to work to fill her spare time.

Finally, some six months later, the house sold. Karen handled the closing by herself. She then made all the moving arrangements and did most of the packing. She even drove across the country with the children. Her move to Kentucky turned out to be a disaster. She disliked living there so much and was so unhappy that she eventually left her husband and returned to Phoenix with the children.

She said that by her handling everything and becoming so independent during the six months they were separated, she knew she could handle things on her own. She blamed her husband's company for not providing better moving arrangements for the family. (Some companies sell the house, so that the family can move together.) She blamed the move itself for the ultimate breakup of their marriage.

"You're really writing a book to help women through the moving process? Huh!" she said when she finished her story. "I could have used something like that to help me when I moved. You know, my husband keeps calling me to come back to Kentucky."

"Oh, really?"

"When you finish that book, do you think you could bring me a copy?"

I smiled. "Of course, I'd love to bring you a copy."

And I walked away knowing God can even use a book on moving to introduce Himself to a woman who needs Him in her life.

Moving Overcomers

No matter where I go, or with whom I talk, it seems everyone has a moving story to share. In each of the stories you've just read, moving has had a different impact on the women who told them. Some experiences have been nicks, some have been dings. With the possible exception of Karen, all these women have an unwavering faith, an inner strength, and an enduring perseverance which allowed them to overcome their obstacles in moving. Their journey of healing varied according to the impact of their move, but they all eventually began to let go, start over, and move ahead with their lives.

Let me tell you, specifically, what makes these women "moving overcomers." Their unwavering faith is in Jesus Christ. Their inner strength comes from Him. Their enduring perseverance is a result of knowing Jesus as their Lord. Their stories are different, but their message is the same. May their journeys as moving overcomers give you hope!

Here are some of their thoughts as they reflect on that journey:

"I rely on God to meet my needs."

"I daily surrender myself and my situation to God."

"I try to look at my circumstances from God's perspective."

"God is my security."

"I spend a lot of time in prayer."

"God's word sustains me."

"I pray about everything."

"I try to remember that God is in control."

"I walk by faith, not by sight."

"God didn't bring us here to go backward."

"I have to let go and trust God."

"He will not leave me nor forsake me."

"I have learned to seek God when there is no one else."

"God brought us here for a purpose. It's enough for me to know that."

Hold Onto the Rope!

Several years ago, my friend Sandy shared with me a wonderful story from *Guideposts* magazine. We have used it many times to help newcomers hold on after a move has caused a ding or a nick to their lives.

The story is a daughter's loving remembrance of her mother. She tells how her mother would refer to a rope that represented her faith in God, and how she would hold onto that rope during hard times. Her mother said, "I felt like a lone mountain climber stranded on the verge of an abyss with no hope, but with the rope coiled on my shoulder. . . . I threw the rope into the void, and it held." She referred to the rope as being woven of thousands of strands threaded with God's goodness, His faithfulness, His word, and most of all, constant prayer. "Pray without ceasing even when you don't feel like it . . . keep weaving that rope," she said.[1]

My friends, I also want you to remember that God "weaves in" His promises, His hope, His everlasting love, and His mercy to strengthen the rope all the more. It cannot be pulled apart. The threads of your life have been woven together into a rope strong enough to carry you. Just remember that when you need it, the rope will hold.

When a friend is moving, I give her a piece of white rope with a pink bow tied around it as a reminder of God's love and tell her to hold onto the rope!

Survival Kit

Scriptures for a "ding" or a "nick" that happen in your move:

"And He is before all things, and in Him all things hold together" (Col. 1:17).

"Trust in the Lord with all your heart, and do not lean on your own understanding. In all your ways acknowledge Him, and He will make your paths straight" (Prov. 3:5-6).

"Pray without ceasing" (I Thess. 5:17).

"Delight yourself in the Lord, and He will give you the desires of your heart. Commit your way to the Lord, trust also in Him, and He will do it" (Psa. 37:4-5).

"And we know that God causes all things to work together for good to those who love God, to those who are called according to His purpose" (Rom. 8:28).

"But if we hope for what we do not see, with perseverance we wait eagerly for it" (Rom. 8:25).

"Do not fear, for I am with you; do not anxiously look about you, for I am your God. I will strengthen you, surely I will help you" (Isa. 41:10).

"Come to Me, all who are weary and heavy-laden, and I will give you rest" (Matt.11:28).

"Though the fig tree should not blossom, and there be no fruit on the vines, though the yield of the olive should fail, and the fields produce no food, though the flock should be cut off from the fold, and there be no cattle in the stalls, yet I will exult in the Lord, I will rejoice in the God of my salvation" (Hab. 3:17-18). (One of my favorites!)

I could go on and on with refreshing scriptures. But perhaps these verses will inspire *you* to dig deeper into God's word.

♥   Heart Talk   ♥

As I reflect on the dings and nicks of moving, I realize that most of us will get bumped along the way. How well we cope determines whether they become dings or nicks! If we're inflexible, the jolt will be severe. If we roll with the punches, adjust and adapt to the bumps of moving, the problems won't be as painful.

Be a moving overcomer and don't let the impact of your bumps cause permanent damage to your life!

Now let's see what you and a suitcase have in common!

Chapter 6

Have Suitcase,
Will Travel

We live with this feeling of being just a beat-up suitcase
that got misrouted somewhere.
Laurie

We've seen that the first step in letting go is dealing with all we've left behind, in learning what to cherish and what to cling to, and in understanding how deeply our move has affected us. Now let's look at the suitcases we carry with us when we move and see how much we resemble them.

Being the people-watcher that I am, airports are especially fascinating to me. They became my hangout during the years that Bill traveled so much in business. I accumulated a lot of "frequent shuttling miles" driving Bill back and forth to the airport. One time, I waited at the gate for five hours through one delay after another. When you're an airport groupie such as I was, you begin to make observations and learn a great deal about travelers.

"Mr. Miller, meet your party in the baggage claim area." Sound familiar? The baggage area seems to be the place everybody ends up. It's the place where they wait . . . and wait . . . and . . . ! I've observed that when people first get off a plane they move quickly toward the baggage area. As I'm watching them, I have just a moment for that first impression. But by the time I arrive at baggage area, they are usually standing around. Then I can take the time to really observe them.

It's obvious that some of those standing around are coming home. They are chatting in an animated way with family and friends. For other passengers, however, this seems to be a new experience. They are entering a new phase of their lives—a new town, a new job, new friends. Everything looks huge and intimidating. Others have come in sorrow—perhaps because of a death or an illness. They wear their emotions like a heavy cloak. For a few, there is a look of anxiety; they are not sure what's ahead for them. And then there are those who are just happy to have reached their destination. They wanted to come, they looked forward to being there, and now they have finally arrived.

It's not too hard to separate the seasoned travelers from the novices, those who are having a familiar experience from those who are in unfamiliar territory. Those who have traveled a lot look either relaxed or bored. Those who are having a first or even second travel experience look agitated and upset.

There's a parallel with moving here. If you've done it before, it's not too tough; but if moving is a new experience, you can count on feeling anxiety, sorrow, relief, and perhaps happiness when you finally reach your destination.

Our Luggage Is a Lot Like Us

I began to watch passengers more closely and noticed how some people looked like their bags! Businessmen and women picked up leather, executive-styled suitcases. A matching designer set of luggage was claimed by a matching couple in matching designer clothes. Golf bags belonged to tanned men wearing knit sport shirts and shorts. Well-coiffured women wearing huge jewelry pulled luggage wrapped in protective vinyl. A large family, with children of all ages, picked up at least eight well-worn bags in all shapes and sizes, with matching ribbons tied to the handles for identification.

I found myself wondering about all of these people, *Does their luggage look on the inside like it does on the outside? Or, does it just represent what they want to look like on the outside, and they keep the inside safely hidden from view?*

As women on the move, much of our identity can be portrayed by how our suitcase—our personhood—looks from the outside.

Just Call Me "The Bag Lady"

I would never think of throwing away my old suitcase. It's very much a part of my life after all these years. It's a friend, an enemy, a traveling companion, a place where I store feelings and emotions, and a keeper of treasures. You might have one just like it—a cheap mustard-colored vinyl bag with a large ugly zipper. It's dusty, worn-out, frazzled, frayed, scarred up, bent in, coming apart at the seams, all with a broken zipper! There have been times in our moves when I felt like I looked like my suitcase. I claimed it then as my identity.

Many of us arrive at our destinations looking like:

Labeled Linda. She's covered with stickers and tags that say *Fragile, Handle with Care, Received Damaged, Transfer to, Transferred from, Final Destination.* Like Linda, in the middle of a move, we're not sure who we are and where we're going. We just know we've lost a major part of our identity.

I'll never forget the pastor's wife who came up to me after I finished speaking to newcomers at a seminar last year. Her eyes were brimming with tears, and she asked if she could talk to me for a moment. There was an urgency in her voice as she said, "We just moved here, and everybody wants a piece of me. Will I teach Sunday School? Will I play the piano? Will I lead a Bible Study? and on and on! Nobody has even asked me how I am, how I am adjusting. They never ask what can they do for me. Talk about feeling labeled! My identity is wrapped up in what they think I can do for them. I just want to pull the covers over my head and stay in bed."

That was the first time I realized the kind of struggle so many pastors' wives have in moving, and yet people in their congregations just expect them to jump in and start serving them. We need to be sensitive to their needs; they have to adjust just like anyone else.

Dusty Doris. She's been stuffed in the closet or pushed under the bed. One Dusty Doris told me in a weary voice, "Moving is so traumatic for me that my husband has stopped asking me about moving again. He doesn't even consider my feelings about another move."

Worn-Out Wilma. She's just so far gone that she can't be put back together again. When I met Wilma in the newcomer's class at our church, the first thing she said to me was, "I'm so tired from this move. I'm exhausted from unpacking and setting up our home. My husband started traveling immediately. That left me with taking care of our four children, and everything else that needed to be done."

Frazzled-and-Frayed Frances. Frances has had so much piled on top of her that she's crying out, "I can't take anymore! Don't ask me to do one more thing until I get unpacked!"

Scarred-Up Suzy. She has been mishandled by life. Divorced and self-supporting with two children, she'd just moved to our town and had come to our church looking for a place to belong. Our newcomers enfolded and encouraged her.

Bent-In Bertha. As I saw her walking toward me, I could tell Bertha was all bent out of shape. All she did was complain. She complained about living in Arizona; she complained about the heat; she complained about the desert. Nothing pleased her. "Why did the company have to move us here?" she whined in a high voice.

Coming-Apart-at-the-Seams Sybil. She's on the verge of losing it. Sybil and her husband had been in Phoenix only six months when he lost his job. Their house payments were already more than they could afford, and if something didn't change quickly, they would lose their home. The stress of it all was beginning to affect their marriage. She said, "I'm falling apart. What will happen to us?"

Zipper-Broken Zelda. She won't open up and she's lost her zip. When she came to our class she sat by herself. Her smile was forced. She didn't say much, but I knew she was hiding behind the pain of her move. It took weeks for her to finally begin to tell her story. She and her husband had moved 10 times in 13 years of marriage. It had become easier for her to remain detached than to open up to new relationships. She looked into my eyes and said, "It's too painful to have to say good-bye again and again."

When I think of suitcases, I can just envision a family luggage set. It might look something like this:

26" Pullman—the father
24" Pullman—the mother
21" Carry-ons—the children
The Hang-up Bag—the teenagers

Where do you fit? Maybe you feel like a 26" Pullman, because you've had to be the heavyweight—the one in charge. Maybe you feel like the carry-on because you had no choice about coming. Maybe you feel like the hang-up bag because of your hang-ups about this move. Or, could it be you don't even feel like a part of the set; instead you feel like a bag that's leftover from other moves?

Go for the Designer Bag

Sometimes, in my weaker moments, I imagine replacing my old mustard-colored vinyl bag, the one with the large ugly zipper, with a new designer bag. I'd like the kind that has an all-over floral-print fabric. Mine would have big cabbage roses in shades of pink and burgundy and wheels that glide through an airport. It would have lots of zippered compartments to put all my special little things in and it would be stain and tear resistant. On the sturdy handle would be a fancy little gold lock that only I could open. Wouldn't that be great? I think designer bags are constructed by someone who obviously knows a lot about luggage and a lot about people.

♥   Heart Talk   ♥

If I could be with you right this moment, we'd have our heart talk and a cup of coffee. This is what I would tell you: Exchange your beat-up old suitcase for a designer bag. Or maybe we should say, the *Designer's* bag! Because what the Designer provides in that bag can be an anchor in your life and in all the moves you'll ever make. You will never have to travel without it again, and the best part of it all is that the Master Designer Himself goes with you.

With your beautiful bag you'll be identified as a woman who trusts God as the Master Designer. He doesn't make mistakes. He's the one who can handle all your moving situations, no matter what they are.

With this designer bag:

You are tagged for the right destination. You know that all the moves during your lifetime are just temporary. Your eternal destination will be permanent.

You are marked with God's "special handling" label. God loves the weary. He cares for the worn-out, frazzled, and frayed. His compassion extends to the scarred-up. His understanding reaches those who are coming apart at the seams. He gives newness to the dusty and bent-in and His wholeness to those who are broken.

You are secure in God's love. Nothing—absolutely nothing, or anything, or any amount of miles—can separate you from the love of God.

You are sturdy. God is holding onto you. He will not let you go!

Scriptures for a Well-Worn Traveler

"And the Lord will continually guide you, and satisfy your desire in scorched places, and give strength to your bones; And you will be like a watered garden, and like a spring of water whose waters do not fail" (Isa. 58:11).

"We look not at the things which are seen, but at the things which are not seen; for the things which are seen are temporal, but the things which are not seen are eternal" (2 Cor. 4:18).

"The Lord is your keeper . . . He will keep your soul. The Lord will guard your going out and your coming in from this time forth and forever" (Psa. 121:5-8).

"I have loved you with an everlasting love" (Jer. 31:3).

"Do not fear, for I have redeemed you; I have called you by name; you are Mine! When you pass through the waters, I will be with you; and through the rivers, they will not overflow you" (Isa. 43:1-2).

"For I am convinced that neither death, nor life, nor angels, nor principalities, nor things present, nor things to come, nor powers, nor height, nor depth, nor any other created thing, shall be able to separate us from the love of God, which is in Christ Jesus our Lord" (Rom. 8:38-39).

In this chapter, we've had a little fun talking about identifying with our suitcases, and finding some interesting labels stuck on us. But how do we feel on the inside? When I opened the suitcase of my life, I found many feelings about our moves and how they had affected me. I had stuffed a lot of emotions inside until after our last move when I finally began to deal with them. I would have liked it better if my feelings and emotions had been neatly folded and packed in my suitcase at each move; but so many times I just threw them in, closed the lid on them, and rushed on to the next move. All the while, my load became heavier and heavier.

What baggage are you still dragging behind you? Can you identify the emotional labels—luggage tags—that are attached to you? In the next chapter, we're going to take a look *inside* your suitcase!

Chapter 7

It's Time to Throw Away Those Luggage Tags!

Then David left his baggage in the care of the baggage keeper.
1 Samuel 17:22

I remember the emotional baggage that I carried after our move to Phoenix. Even though the physical baggage I brought with me had long since been unpacked, I still had emotional baggage stuffed away that hadn't even been opened after our move. These were emotions and feelings that I needed to identify and work through in order to start over and move ahead. I struggled with comparing myself with others. I struggled with feelings of inadequacy and discouragement. And I struggled with the biggest one of all, *loss of identity!*

Southern sundresses, homes with basements and attics, BIG yards, the word *y'all*, and the beauty of four seasons were suddenly compared with the jeans-and-boots look, no extra storage space, my "dog run" yard, the phrase *you guys*, and one, long, hot summer!

In the areas where I once felt adequate, I now felt extremely inadequate. I used to be able to zip around town in no time, knowing just where to go for what I needed. Then we moved and I had no idea where I was going; I just hoped I was going to end up at the right place and be home before dark! I had always been so verbal and such a "take charge" person. Then we moved and I became strangely quiet and would find myself sitting in the back row at church. I was discouraged with my new life, and yearned for a friend who *really* knew me.

Yet, I can say that with the magic of time, a change of attitude, and a redirected focus on God, I love living here. This is where my home and my heart are.

In Chapter 6 we talked about how some women look like their suitcases on the outside. In this chapter, we are going to affix luggage tags that will label the feelings contained inside those suitcases. Now that I've identified some of my feelings and emotions, let's take a closer look at others that might be all too familiar to you.

Identify Your Own Luggage Tags

Here are some "luggage tags" you might be wearing since your move:

Anger. Are you harboring anger because you didn't want to move?

Bitterness. Do you feel bitter because this move has caused major changes in your life?

Comparison. Do you find yourself comparing everything to where you used to live?

Fear. Are you afraid you'll never again feel that sense of belonging and security?

Anxiety. Are you anxious about making new friends and finding the right school, church, doctor, grocery store, cleaners, and hairdresser?

Disappointment. Is the house not what you really wanted? Is the job a disillusionment? Is the cost of living higher?

Loss of Identity. Has your self-esteem taken a nose-dive? Have you gotten lost in the shuffle?

Depression. Is everything overwhelming and you'd rather stay in bed than unpack a box, hang a picture, or fix a meal?

Expectations. Were you expecting the neighbors to be friendly? To find a close friend soon? To be included?

Inadequacy. Do you feel as if you just don't have what it takes anymore?

Hurt. Do the tears come when you think of family and friends you left behind?

Grief. Are you grieving over all your losses?

(You can probably even come up with a list of your own!)

She Hates the Weather and the Bugs

Margaret moved away from Virginia and now is miserable in Iowa, longing to be back in her former home. She is still wearing so many luggage tags, and is still in so much pain from her move, that she's leading a life of misery and despair. The fact is, six months after their move she still hasn't adjusted, and it's having a ripple effect upon her children and her marriage. She harbors great anger and bitterness toward her husband for moving them to Iowa. Even though they bought a new home and had it beautifully decorated and landscaped, even though they are going to a great church nearby, and even though she has everything that would appear to make her happy, she said to me not long ago, "I hate it here; my life is so empty. There isn't anything about this place I like."

She told me that she hates the weather and that the bugs are terrible. When I asked her children how *they* like living there, they said, "It's always raining, and the bugs are everywhere!" See the ripple effect? Young children mirror what they see and hear within the home. Then they begin to have those same feelings.

Margaret's marriage is also drifting apart. She resents Sam for being so busy with his new job. "He doesn't seem to have time for me anymore, and we used to be inseparable." They no longer have any quality time alone when Sam isn't working. Any leftover time goes to the children and their activities. It seems Margaret and Sam live in two separate worlds, and the distance between them is growing. Margaret is still wearing the luggage tags of anger, bitterness, and resentment that have kept her from starting over and moving forward with her life.

Are you still wearing luggage tags? Which ones? What feelings and emotions are keeping you from starting over and going forward after your move? This is the best time to stop and take a good look at those tags—to identify them one by one, acknowledge what they are doing to you and your family, and make the choice to remove them. You may not know how or where to begin the process, so here are some steps to help you get started.

David Can Show You How

I have often compared our luggage tags of today with the story of David and Goliath in the Bible. David had to overcome Goliath, the giant in his life, just as you must overcome the "giants" you face daily, such as anger, fear, bitterness, discouragement, and disappointment. Whatever your giant luggage tags might be, there is much to learn from David. (See 1Samuel 17.) Let's take a look at the story.

David left his baggage in the care of the Baggage Keeper, God (v. 22). He left behind the things that would encumber him and keep him from getting to the battle line to see his brothers. Doing this is vital as you choose to:

Let go,
　　Start over,
　　　　Move ahead with your life.

- Leave your baggage in the care of God, the Baggage Keeper. In other words, let go of the emotional baggage you're still carrying—those feelings that are keeping you in bondage. Leave them in the hands of the One who loves you and who can heal you, Jesus Christ.
- Rely on God's faithfulness (v. 37). Just as David recalled God's faithfulness to him in the past, recall the times of God's faithfulness in your own life. Be specific.
- Be yourself. Don't try to be someone else! In verses 38-39, David realized that the garments Saul clothed him with weren't right for him; so he took them off and went to face Goliath just as he was—a shepherd boy with five stones and a sling. When you move to a new place, face your transition in the beauty of who God made you to be. Don't try to be who others think you should be, or try to blend in by acting like everyone else.
- Be equipped. Take five smooth stones (v. 40) to face the giants:
  1. Faith. Have the kind of faith David had when he reached down in the brook for five stones, knowing that killing the giant was an impossible task without God's help. He recognized his own weakness but had the faith to know he could face Goliath with God's strength.

2. Prayer. Don't even attempt to stand up to your giants until you go down on your knees in prayer! You can't fight anger with anger, but you can fight anger with prayer.
3. Bible study. The more you know and study God's word, the firmer the ground upon which you stand will be! God's word will keep you on track with His truth and His promises.
4. Fellowship. Seek out the fellowship of Christian friends—for support, for accountability, for group Bible study, for encouragement, for fun! Great strength lies in numbers. It's important not to feel alone as we face the obstacles that we need to overcome.
5. Perseverance. Keep on keeping on! Don't give up and don't give in. David didn't give up in spite of Goliath's size and strong voice of intimidation and belittling (vv. 43-44). What voices are you hearing that tell that you can't do it, that you can't overcome your giants?

Here are three more important ideas to help you win against the giants:

- Be not afraid "for the battle is the Lord's" (vv. 45,47). Your part, like David's, is to be willing, to be prepared, and to be confident in the Lord!
- Be quick! "David ran quickly toward the battle line" (v. 48). Don't delay in confronting the giant in your life that's hurting you, your husband, your children, or your relationship with God.
- Be bold! "David put his hand into his bag and took from it a stone and slung it" (v. 49). Then he trusted God for the results! Trust God with all your heart, with all your soul, and with all your might for the results! Pick up your stones and take action!

I shared all of this with my friend Margaret the last time I saw her. She cried as she began to recognize the luggage tags that were still attached to her from her move. She cried and I just held her, listening as she talked. (Listening is one of the greatest gifts you can give a newcomer like Margaret. She yearns to speak her thoughts and have someone interested enough to listen.)

"I see what's been happening to me," she said. "I see how I've held onto this anger at Sam for moving us here and how it's built walls between us. For the first time, I'm really seeing how negative the children have become. I've resented the time Sam puts into work; yet I know it's all part of this new promotion."

Slowly, she began to identify the pain in her life. We talked again about "leaving your baggage with the Baggage Keeper" and how you can "Cast your burden upon the Lord and He will sustain you" (Psa. 55:22).

"You can leave all this baggage, all these luggage tags of pain, all these giants that cast a shadow over your life at the feet of Jesus," I told Margaret. "Just pick up your stones and take action!" I caught a glimpse of hope in her eyes. I knew this was a turning point in her life. I suggested she and Sam make time to go out to dinner, go for a walk, go on a picnic—anything—as long as she could talk to him and start sharing her feelings. It was clear that Margaret had not told Sam how she was feeling, and the longer she kept her emotions inside, the more hardened she became.

Margaret did a rather clever thing. She met Sam on his own turf. She made a lunch appointment with him, writing it in his Daytimer, and began a once-a-week-set-aside-time-for-me opportunity to talk that eventually helped Sam understand the changes that had taken place in his wife since they had moved. Now he understood why he had been feeling so rejected. The rejection had caused him to work harder and longer. The lunches have since become evenings out, and the walls are coming down between them.

Margaret is seeking the positive rather than the negative in their new city. She's beginning to discover the uniqueness that Iowa has to offer. She and the children are making a scrapbook of "Things to Do and Places to Go" for the children's grandparents in Virginia.

"Don't just go to church, Margaret," I told her, "get *involved* in church! Join a women's Bible study, a couples' small group Bible study, or a Sunday School class." I knew that in a small group setting she would begin to make friends and form relationships. Margaret called me the other day to say that with time, a change of attitude, and a redirected focus on God, her life is changing and she is moving beyond her pain.

"Yes," I said, smiling as my eyes filled with tears of joy, "I understand exactly what you mean!" Many of you face the same circumstances as Margaret and can relate as well.

Each time you move, you acquire a new kind of luggage tag. The important thing is to not allow those labels to misdirect you and keep sending you back into pain. You will face giants daily, whether you move or not. It's critical to recognize and acknowledge what the "giant" luggage tags are, come face to face with them, and then:

- Leave your baggage with the Baggage Keeper.
- Rely on God's faithfulness.

- Be who you are.
- Be equipped.
- Don't be afraid.
- Be quick.
- Be bold.
- Trust God for the results!

I wanted Jean to pull off the luggage tags of feelings and emotions that could easily become giants in her life. I suggested that she copy this list and keep it handy for reference.

Replace the Luggage Tags

Anger or bitterness with forgiveness

"Let all bitterness . . . and anger . . . be put away from you . . . forgiving each other, just as God in Christ also has forgiven you" (Eph. 4:31-32).

Comparison with contentment

"For we are not bold to class or compare ourselves" (2 Cor. 10:12).

"For I have learned to be content in whatever circumstances I am" (Phil. 4:11).

Fear with courage

"Do not fear, for I am with you; do not anxiously look about you, for I am your God" (Isa. 41:10).

"When I am afraid, I will put my trust in Thee" (Psa. 56:3).

Anxiety with assurance

"Do not be anxious for your life, as to what you shall eat, or what you shall drink; nor for your body, as to what you shall put on" (Matt. 6:25-26).

"Casting all your anxiety upon Him, because He cares for you" (1 Pet. 5:7).

Disappointment with fulfillment

"Now to Him who is able to do exceeding abundantly beyond all that we ask or think, according to the power that works within us" (Eph. 3:20).

Loss of identity with security

"I have called you by name; you are Mine! Since you are precious in My sight" (Isa. 43:1,4).

"If I take the wings of the dawn, if I dwell in the remotest part of the sea, even there Thy hand will lead me, and Thy right hand will lay hold of me" (Psa. 139:9-10).

Depression with hope

"Now may the God of hope fill you with all joy and peace" (Rom. 15:13)

"For my hope is from Him. He only is my rock and my salvation, my stronghold; I shall not be shaken" (Psa. 62:5-6).

Read the entire Book of Psalms!

Discouragement with encouragement

"That through perseverance and the encouragement of the Scriptures we might have hope" (Rom. 15:4).

"And the Lord is the one who goes ahead of you; He will be with you. He will not fail you or forsake you. Do not fear, or be dismayed" (Deut. 31:8).

Expectations with gratitude

"Set your mind on the things above, not on the things that are on earth" (Col. 3:2).

"Every good thing bestowed and every perfect gift is from above" (James 1:17).

Inadequacy with confidence

"For the Lord will be your confidence, and will keep your foot from being caught" (Prov. 3:26).

Hurt with comfort

"The Father of mercies and God of all comfort; who comforts us in all our affliction so that we may be able to comfort those who are in any affliction . . . our comfort is abundant through Christ" (2 Cor. 1:3-5).

Grief with comfort

"My soul weeps because of grief; strengthen me according to Thy word" (Psa. 119:28).

♥   Heart Talk   ♥

My dear new friends, the one thing to remember, from this day forward, now and always: The only luggage tag you will want to wear, that you will want to claim as your own, is the one that says, "I am a child of God!"

Now that we've come this far together, I hope you consider me a friend as well; someone who understands and cares about you. Continue to let go and allow God to mend you. Hold this verse in your heart, "I can do all things through Him who strengthens me" (Phil. 4:13).

I'm excited about getting into the next section in which we begin the Starting Over process. Where do we begin? Within ourselves, within our homes, and within our families.

PART II

Start Over

In Part One, we walked through the process of letting go. It's my prayer that you have let go of any encumbrances preventing you from starting over and moving ahead with your life. If you have not let go, decide right now to let God mend you so you can be the whole, happy, and productive woman He wants you to be. Choose to be open to His love and healing, and when you do, you'll be ready to start over.

To start over, you'll need to give attention to four areas:

- Build your nest by making the house you've moved into your home.
- Recognize the effects moving has had on your children.
- Keep your marriage ties strong.
- Deal with the personal issues of loneliness, lack of self-esteem, and your need for new friends.

Remember to bloom where you are planted. Remember that letting go allows God to mend you. And remember, starting over allows God to mold you!

Chapter 8

Building Your Nest

Anybody can build a house; we need the Lord
for the creation of a home.
John Henry Jowett

A s women, the first thing we want to do as we start over is to build our
nest again. As part of that process, what our family does when we
move into a house is to immediately put up our hammock. The last thing
we do before moving out is to take it down.

For as long as I can remember, a hammock has been a part of my life and
home. As a child, part of the anticipation of going to Grandmother's house
included running up the steps to the big front porch and jumping into the
hammock where I could swing to my heart's content. Mama and Daddy had
one for our family, and now we continue to pass the hammock tradition on
to the next generation. The hammock has become a symbol of home to our
family.

The kind of hammock we have is a large crisscross, white cotton rope swing that hooks to two large trees. Two people can lie in the hammock at the same time, or more than two people can sit in it and swing as long as they like. Now that you can picture my hammock, let's pretend that we are swinging in it. We can visit together, and I will share with you the first thing you need to know as you build your *new* nest.

The Nest Builders

One day I noticed part of the rope on my hammock was loose and hanging down. Since this had never happened before, I took a closer look. Obviously, the rope had frayed at the end, causing it to weaken and come loose. *How this could have happened?* I wondered. And so I watched closely throughout the day. Much to my amazement, I saw two little birds fly down and pull at the rope end until they had pulled a piece loose! They flew off with the fragments in their mouths to a thick honeysuckle vine growing up the wall of our house. I quietly peeked through the vine to discover a nest made of *my hammock rope!* The birds had crafted a nest of rope mixed with grass and twigs. Being the bird lover that I am (I've always felt that one of my missions in life is to feed every bird that regularly stops in my yard), I didn't disturb the nest. I just moved the hammock from its prime location to another spot.

As I watched the mama bird and her babies in their nest, I was reminded of similar ways we can "nest" in our new homes. We have to start with quality "nest-building materials" to give our home a firm foundation. There are four things I want to pass on to you about the nest-building process.

1. The materials to use in building your nest are love, joy, peace, patience, kindness, goodness, faithfulness, gentleness, (and) self-control (Gal. 5:22-23).

All these materials will become part of the fiber of your nest, as a result of knowing and loving Jesus Christ. They are the inner qualities that you practice, not preach, in your home. It is *who* you are, rather than *what* you can do. God will work in you to bring about a Christ-likeness in your life, and that Christ-likeness will ultimately be reflected in the lives of your family members.

A friend once told me after we had talked about nest-building, "I'm so glad God gives us second chances when we move. I needed to weave more peace and patience into our home. I let my circumstances control me, instead of letting God control me. The last time we moved, we were hurting financially and I took my frustration out on the children. Our circumstances haven't changed, but my attitude has. I want to do it differently this time."

She realized her own inadequacies, and the difference it would make in her personality and in her home if she let God control her life.

As a woman, you have an enormous amount of influence in your home. You are the pivotal point. You are the catalyst for what happens there. My dear friend and Southern soul-sister, Sudie, always says, "If Mama ain't happy, ain't nobody happy!" How true it is! As you weave the essence of who you are into your nest, your attitudes and actions will spill over to affect your husband and children. If you are frazzled, your home will appear frazzled. If you are peaceful, your home will reflect your peace. If you are happy, other family members will be too, for happiness is contagious. If you yell and scream, that too can be contagious. The strongest nest-building material available to you is Christ in you. He will weave Himself through you and about you and He will strengthen your whole family.

2. It doesn't matter what kind of nest you have; the important thing is that you make that nest a home. Some birds live in fancy birdhouses and others in nests of twigs. Your nest may be a house, an apartment, a patio home, a condo, or a trailer. A lot of women will say to me, "But I don't have a house; I live in an apartment, and that's not a home. Why should I even try to fix it up?" The place you live is an extension of yourself, the essence of who you are. It reveals your identity.

Take Stephanie, for example. She and her husband live with their baby in a trailer. Their trailer home is truly a place of loveliness. Pots of flowers on the porch greet visitors. The eat-in kitchen has a bow window with colorful curtains. On the table are fresh flowers. Stephanie has decorated each room economically and attractively and made it a warm and inviting haven. Her home reveals who she is and expresses what she believes. My friend loves being a wife and mother, and she has learned to be content in her circumstances. Stephanie reflects the peace and joy that comes from her strong relationship with God. It is obvious that the presence of Christ lives in their home, and that love and faith are woven into their nest for a firm foundation.

3. Some birds don't stay in one place very long; they vacate their nests and move on. Yet, no matter how long a bird occupies a nest, she makes it a warm and cozy home for her family. It is her number one priority.

Take a lesson from the birds. Even if you are in your nest for only a few weeks, months, or just a year before moving on, make the effort to settle in and make it a home for your family. You will never regret the effort.

In our mobile society there are many short-term assignments, and unless we make nest-building a priority, it's easy to neglect. Large companies, the civil service, or the military, just to name a few, routinely move families every one or two years.

When Bill was in the Air Force, we lived in a one-bedroom, efficiency apartment for less than a year. It would have been so easy to not unpack the boxes containing our pictures and accessories. After all, we weren't going to be there for long, so what difference would it make? The difference was that Bill and I needed a place to belong, regardless of how short our stay might be. I decided that wherever we were living, I would always make a home for us. I'd put out the welcome mat, put a plant by the front door, and arrange either inexpensive flowers from the grocery store or fresh greenery from outside on the kitchen table. Then I'd hang the pictures and place the accessories around the house. That way, no matter where we lived, when Bill walked in the front door he would feel he had come home.

After the children came, I continued the same practice. It was important that the children be able to connect their old home with the new one. It speeded up their process of putting down roots.

Dear moving friends, don't ever think *temporary*. The imprint of a home today will make a lasting impression for tomorrow in the lives of all who live in your house.

4. The last observation I made about those little birds outside my house, was how much order there was in their nest. It was obvious the nest was there to provide shelter, security, food, and a safe place to grow. The young all lined up with their tiny mouths open, and just sat there in a row, waiting to be fed. They depended on their mother to take care of them.

No matter how disorganized and temporary you may feel, your family looks to you to provide their daily needs of security, encouragement and nurturing love.

What is the condition of your nest? Is there order or confusion? Remember, "God is not a God of confusion!" (1 Cor. 14:33). Your home will be "ordered by God," if you put your trust in Him, place your security in Him, depend on Him to meet your needs, and base your values on His word. It all goes back to being Christ-centered in your life and in your home. When you are, you will then be equipped to feed your family with biblical truths and provide the tools they need for growth.

You Are Not Forgotten

I am sensitive to the particular circumstances of many of my moving friends. First of all, my heart is heavy when I realize that an overwhelming number of you are single parents who have carried all the responsibilities for your home, even when moving. Moving is a physical and emotional strain on *anyone*, let alone someone who is trying to do it *solo*.

Perhaps you're a single mother who has thought after completing the move, *I don't have a husband, so why make a home? I don't have any reason to build a nest.* Oh, but you do, you have the very best reason of all—your children. Your children need to experience, on a daily basis, the nest-building qualities of love, acceptance, security, affirmation, and accountability. They need to see that your life is centered on Christ and not your circumstances. They need to know they are not alone and that they can make the transition to this new home. God will help them and He will help you, too!

If you are a single person with no children, and are making a move, let me remind you that you, too, are not alone. Christ can and will fill your home and your heart with a peace and a fullness that come only from a relationship with Him. When you are settling in, build your nest bright and beautiful. Make a safe home for yourself. Make it a place where you can welcome new friends.

Others of you may be married, but you feel as if you're moving alone because your husband doesn't share your faith. Even if only one person in a family knows Jesus Christ, reflects His love, and weaves a nest with Christlike qualities, change can come to the unbelievers in the family. If you are that one person, your part is to keep believing and keep weaving.

Weaving the Fruit of the Spirit into Your Nest

After you've woven the basics, the physical comforts, into your nest, how do you go on strengthening it? By incorporating the nine fruits of the Spirit.

Love

Love "bears all things, believes all things, hopes all things, endures all things" (1 Cor. 13:7).

Love is the main material from which to weave your new nest. Those things which express love don't necessarily have to be huge acts of kindness. It's often the little things that say "I love you." Things like:

A smile
A hug
A touch
A word of encouragement
A word of praise
A word of affirmation
A love note that reads, "I'm so glad we're all here together as we start
    over."

For a time after you move, family members may be a little fragile and
may need an extra measure of tender, loving care. Let love permeate your
home like the fragrance of perfume.

*How can you demonstrate an observable love to your husband, children, and
friends? By expressing . . .*

Joy

"These things I have spoken to you, that My joy may be in you,
and that your joy may be made full" (Jn. 15:11).

Joy is an attitude and a choice we make. We shouldn't let our joy depend
on circumstances; rather, we can have joy in spite of our circumstances.

A moving friend said, "This wasn't the house I wanted. We don't have a
yard, and there isn't any money left to buy curtains." She said it without
whining or acting upset. She continued, "I knew, however, my attitude
about what I didn't have would affect my whole family, so I just decided to
make the best of the situation. I dwelt on the positives about the house, put
my plants outside in pots, and got some colorful sheets to make curtains!"

In which of your circumstances do you need to choose joy?

Peace

"And the peace of God, which surpasses all comprehension, shall
guard your hearts and your minds in Christ Jesus" (Phil. 4:7).

Fear will rob you of peace. And a lack of peace will bring anxiety and
worry. But God's peace will protect your heart, mind, emotions, and
thoughts. Without inner tranquillity, you can't weave strength and stability
into your new home.

Chris confessed to me, "I'm so afraid to stay in this house alone when my
husband travels. If something happened, who would I call in the middle of the
night? We don't know anyone yet and the nearest neighbor is a mile away."

That's the kind of worry that creates fear, brings anxiety, and robs you of peace. It's not worthy of one who trusts in Christ.

What are the situations in which you need Christ's peace?

Patience

"We can rejoice, too, when we run into problems and trials for we know that they are good for us—they help us learn to be patient. And patience develops strength of character in us and helps us trust God more each time we use it, until finally our hope and faith are strong and steady" (Rom. 5:3-4, LB).

God taught me more about patience when He had me in a holding pattern, than at any other time in my life. The holding pattern occurred when we were waiting for our house in Atlanta to sell. It didn't sell until 18 months after we arrived in Phoenix. We were strapped with two house payments, and there was nothing we could do but be patient and wait.

Some of you are in a holding pattern as well, and all you can do is wait. Patience allows God to fulfill His plan for you. It's watching God develop His character in you through the circumstances of your move. It's enduring without complaining.

I must say that building a nest with patience was not easy for me then, but in the end I learned to trust God all the more.

When was the last time your patience was tested?

Kindness

"And be kind to one another, tender-hearted, forgiving each other, just as God in Christ also has forgiven you" (Eph. 4:32).

Kindness begins in your home and then spills over beyond it. I'll never forget the time I was busy making cookies for our Newcomer's Coffee. Ginger, my daughter, came into the kitchen just in time to see me put them on a tray. "Great, Mom! You made cookies for us!" she said, as she reached for one. Oops! Guess you know how I felt as I told her they were going to church. Guess you know the message that was conveyed to her—that my kindness went first to others and then to my family. Wrap your own nest in kindness before you pour it everywhere else.

What act of kindness can you show your children today?

Goodness

"Surely goodness and lovingkindness will follow me all the days of my life, and I will dwell in the house of the Lord forever" (Psa. 23:6).

There is a saying that goes, "What you *do* speaks so loudly, that I can't hear what you *say*!" The way we live our lives is the best advertisement for goodness. Goodness characterizes a person of moral excellence, worth, honesty, integrity, virtue, honor, and generosity. What you do and how you live inside your home speaks volumes to your children. They see the real you behind closed doors, and your life is their greatest teacher.

What have you taught about goodness by your example?

Faithfulness
"For we walk by faith, not by sight" (2 Cor. 5:7).

To me, faith is an unwavering confidence in God's word and in His promises. Faith is believing, trusting, and knowing without seeing. You weave your nest every day by faith. I have a small poster on the mirror in my bathroom that says, "Faith isn't faith until it's all you've got left." Sometimes faith is all you have left. I've learned that my faith is enough.

How have you demonstrated your faith in action this week?

Gentleness
"But let it be the hidden person of the heart, with the imperishable quality of a gentle and quiet spirit, which is precious in the sight of God" (1 Pet. 3:4).

A friend shared, "When I moved into the neighborhood, my neighbor was so gentle with me. She had moved six months before and was sensitive to my needs. I'll always remember her gentleness in handling my delicate emotions."

Weave your nest carefully with thoughtfulness, consideration, respect, and courtesy. Gentleness is shown in how we treat others. It is love refined through our actions.

In what way can you enhance gentleness in your life?

Self-Control
"A gentle answer turns away wrath, but a harsh word stirs up anger" (Prov. 15:1).

It doesn't take long for outbursts of anger, quick judgments and bad attitudes to overshadow all the positive things you've built into your nest. I can't tell you the number of times I've blown it by overreacting! Where was everybody when I needed help unpacking the boxes? Boy, did I let them have it! Why wasn't Bill home in time for dinner? Was his new job that important? Well, I sure told him! What did I care if their rooms were never straightened or fixed up! See if it bothered me!

In what ways do you struggle with self-control?

As you begin to build a foundation for your new home, reflect on the nest-building qualities you want to add that may never have existed in your old home.

Over the years, I have always given friends who are moving, or newcomers to my town, a little bird nest with tiny colored eggs in it. It serves as a reminder for them to build their nest with all the fruits of the Spirit included. After years of giving these nests, it's heartwarming when I visit friends' homes, to see those little nests sitting on windowsills or kitchen counters, and to know they have built their nests well.

♥   Heart Talk   ♥

A great word picture for you to remember when creating your home comes from Sylvia Fair's book for children, *The Bedspread*. She tells the wonderful story of two old sisters, Maud and Amelia, who decide to decorate their long white bedspread by embroidering it. Each works from an end as they create pictures of the house they lived in as children.

As they start to embroider, Maud says, "And we'll begin at the front door." Then Amelia says with a smile, "A very good place to start, dear." As the design began to take shape, Maud realizes she's left something out of her intricate stitching. She says to Amelia, "Your house is happy. I forgot to add the happiness." [1]

So, always remember, the best place to start creating a home is at the front door, with a smile, and don't forget to add the happiness! (And I know where you can get a great swing in a hammock, too!)

Let's turn away from feeding the birds and learn how you can bloom where you're planted!

Survival Kit

Twenty ways to build your nest and to make your house a home:

1. Put a welcome mat at the front door.
2. Start a tradition with something that symbolizes home to you and your family. When you move, put it out first; when you leave, take it down last, like my hammock!
3. Buy a flowering plant for the kitchen, the first time you go to the grocery store.

4. Make a list of "wanna-do's" for each room. Keep the list with you. It's amazing how you forget when you are out shopping!

5. Remember when you are decorating, less is more.

6. Keep a 3x5 card-file by your phone as a place to list resources. When someone recommends a service (florist, hairdresser, cleaners), jot the information down to file, or drop a business card in your file.

7. Go for a new look! Don't be a creature of habit. Just because you did it that way before doesn't mean you have to do it that way this time! Arrange the furniture differently. Add a new accent color.

8. Rearrange your accessories.

9. When you meet your neighbors, write their names and house numbers down so you won't forget who lives where. Call them by name the next time you see them.

10. Keep measurements, fabric swatches, paint chips, wallpaper clippings in an envelope in the glove compartment. Be prepared for a decorating sale!

11. Remember—a room looks more interesting if you mix different kinds of furniture and accessories instead of having everything match.

12. Don't overdo your decorating. You can always add something later.

13. Don't try too hard to impress with expensive furniture and accessories, just because you're new in town. Shop at flea markets, thrift shops, and antique malls for best buys!

14. Group things in three's or five's.

15. Baskets! Baskets! Baskets! For magazines, books, plants, fruit, towels, pictures, cards, or great show-off stuff!

16. Burn a scented candle in the kitchen or the bathroom.

17. Start a collection of something you love—teacups, boxes, hat pins, hats, old books, spoons, plates, dolls—anything!

18. Create a home that's comfortable and inviting—not a "show and tell" home, but a "touch and feel" home.

19. Buy different sizes and shapes of picture frames to display your snapshots. Put them in every room. You can never have too many pictures of smiling faces!

20. Put a wreath on the front door.

Finally, don't forget to add the happiness!

Chapter 9

Bloom Where You Are Planted!

Many of us refuse to grow where we are put;
consequently, we take root nowhere.
Oswald Chambers

Have you ever planted flowers in your yard and moved before you got to see them bloom? I have! One year I planted flowers in Georgia and by the time they bloomed the next year, I was planting flowers in North Carolina. I learned from that experience to plant only annuals!

As much as I love birds for the nesting they represent, I love flowers because they help me put down roots wherever I live. I can be the "little old lady in a shoe" and as long as I can plant a posy, I'll be happy. I have had a big yard, a little yard, and now, no yard. But I've always had flowers growing, either in the ground or in pots.

Presently, we live in a patio home with only a concrete pad off the kitchen for a yard. But, you should see it! I went to Home Depot and bought $25.00 worth of bedding plants. I planted them in clay pots, and arranged them in groups of three or five. My patio is beautiful. It provides me with cut flowers for the kitchen, and gives me the feeling of putting down roots.

But that's not all. Outside my window I hung two bird feeders that draw a crowd of supporters, even as I write. The flowers in my hanging basket and the birds who feed outside are like dear friends who cheer me along through each chapter.

I know that moving is a confusing, uprooting time. If I could reach out and touch you right now, I'd give you a big hug. I know how deeply you long to feel rooted and secure. Consider me your cheerleader on the sidelines, encouraging you along with each new chapter in your life. Now, let's begin to break new ground together!

Breaking New Ground

I love asparagus ferns. They require little care and will grow in either the sun or the shade. The only thing you have to remember is that they easily become pot bound. The roots crowd until there is no room for growth. They can even take over the soil. When this happens to my ferns, I have to take the plant out of the pot, put it in a larger one, and add fresh soil and fertilizer. You always know that repotting is successful when the fern gets greener and new growth appears.

A moving friend, Alice, is married to a man who is an airline pilot. They had lived comfortably in Dallas for eight years. Their root system was heavily intertwined with family, friends, and church. But during an airline cutback, he lost his job. Alice was devastated. She knew they would be forced to move in order for her husband to get another job.

Their move brought them to Phoenix. A year later she said to me, "I thought my world had come to an end. I didn't want to leave Dallas. We were so happy and comfortable there. When we came to Phoenix, I was miserable for about six months. Then, we got involved in a great church that made an impact on our lives through the teaching of God's word. We've made wonderful friends through our church and we even host a small group Bible study in our home. My husband makes more money at his new job, flies less, and now he's home with us more than he used to be. I even have a chance to fulfill my dream of going back to college. This move has turned into a blessing in our life!"

Their move was a forced transplant, much like the move of the fern to a bigger pot. But because Alice and her husband were forced out of their comfort zone, they were put into a situation which gave them more room to grow. Their new roots were enriched by the teaching they received from God's word, the Christian friends they met, and their new lifestyle. It was obvious to Alice, when she looked back over the life changes they had made during that first year, that they had been transplanted by God's hand. She had experienced the normal shock of adjustment, but then realized that all the seeds for new growth had come as a result of being uprooted and breaking new ground.

I haven't forgotten those of you who break new ground alone. You are among the growing number of "single movers" who uproot and seek new soil. The single woman who is moving for a job opportunity or to further her education may welcome her transplant as a new challenge and a new experience. The single parent may be looking for a fresh start and a way to distance herself from old memories and surroundings. In either case, however, moving can be twice as hard and stressful when you are alone. The question many single women ask is not, "Why am I moving?" but rather, "How am I going to move by myself?"

Transplanting is much harder without additional hands to help till the soil. A single mover is just as eager as the rest of us to put down her roots and bloom where she's planted. What does she go through when she moves? The feelings and emotions are the same for all women; only the circumstances are different.

My friend Christine is a family and adoption counselor who has moved four times by herself. "Coming home to an empty house every night is the hardest thing for me," she said. "When you're new to a group, it's also very frightening to walk into a room of strangers by yourself." Christine suggests three things that helped her when she moved "Reach out to other single women who may feel the same way you do; find a church and get involved in a small group; and look for community programs that offer activities you are interested in."

At age 22, Julie left her family and friends in Wisconsin to teach school in Phoenix. "The hardest thing for me was that I had no history here. No one knew me. The best thing was that it gave me the opportunity to live life on my own. I wasn't responsible for anyone else." Julie continued, "The first thing I did was to look for a church home to get involved in. I also realized people weren't necessarily going to come up to me, so I sought out other new teachers like myself." Then she said very firmly, "The important thing is, DON'T GIVE UP!"

After her divorce, Marty had to go to work full time. She needed to simplify her life, so she sold her house and moved in order to have a less complicated lifestyle. It was difficult to break old ties and leave old friends. Even though she felt it was essential to move, Marty said wisely, "If you can afford to stay where you are, don't make any changes when children are involved. They are already going through enough transitions."

Leslie is on the Campus Crusade staff and trains missionaries to go all over the world. She has moved six times and even had a cross-cultural adjustment to make when she moved to the Philippines. "Because I'm on the move, I've always rented a place to live," she said. "The hardest thing for me is that I'm never able to accumulate furniture or possessions. Somehow it's just not practical for me to drag those things around from place to place. Moving has taught me to keep my possessions simple, to learn how to adapt, and to have a less complicated life!"

Leslie believes that attitude and choice make a difference when she moves. She has an attitude of hope, knowing God's plan for her move is good. She chooses to bloom where she's planted.

Leslie continued to share some wonderful advice and insight, "As a single woman, I have a need to be around families—so I adopt a family! It's fun to be included and be a part of their lives for special occasions. When I'm lonely, I try to get beyond myself by reaching out to others in need. I've learned that people are willing to help, if you just ask. Don't be afraid to ask for help at your job and at your church. We can't wait for it to happen; we have to make a place for ourselves."

God worked in the lives of these women whether their move was planned or unexpected, welcomed or unwanted. New growth has come to each of them as the women have been uprooted, and have persevered to break new ground alone.

Often, God initiates a move to take you out of your comfort zone and allow you to grow in your relationship with Him. Are you starting to see the great possibilities of your new life in your "new pot"?

How Does Your Garden Grow?

Are you watering your woes or fertilizing your faith? It's easy to water your woes when:

- You can't see the big picture.
- You can't see instant results.
- You can't see the sun shining.
- You don't have the right tools.

Believe me, I have watered my woes many times! When we moved to Phoenix, I couldn't even begin to see the big picture of what God was going to do in my life. I couldn't foresee the depth to which He was going to nurture my growth and cause me to bloom! So, I started watering my woes. I wanted instant results, and when our house in Atlanta didn't sell, my woes reached flood level. Even though it's sunny in Phoenix almost all year long, I couldn't feel the sunshine in my life for months after we moved. My transplant was very difficult for me, and emotionally, I was in deep root-shock for about a year.

Then, I began to see the big picture and understand that our move was God's plan to bring us closer to Him. During the 18 months that we made two house payments, God was teaching us to trust Him and to depend on Him completely. Somehow, every month God provided and the money stretched. As I saw God's faithfulness in our lives, I started to feel the warmth of the sun, and began to adjust to being transplanted. My attitude became more positive and my heart more thankful.

Then, God supplied just the right tools for me to take care of my garden. He gave me a wonderful church home, a nurturing Bible study, and a fellowship of Christian women who came alongside me during the replanting time. My faith became fertilized.

If I made the transition from oak trees to cactus, if I learned to grow green grass in the desert, *you can too!* No matter where you are transplanted, press on to know the Lord, because, "His going forth is as certain as the dawn; and He will come to us like the rain, like the spring rain watering the earth" (Hos. 6:3).

Growing Deeper Roots

What is the purpose of soil? How do you select the best kind? Soil surrounds the plant and provides support. It nourishes the roots and provides chemicals and food for growth. The soil surrounding our lives is God. He surrounds us with His love, provides support through His people, nourishes us through His word, and in Him our roots can grow deep and we can develop to fulfill our potential.

Now is the time to think about the kind of soil you want to surround your life as you are putting down roots. When you move, you have the opportunity to start over and make different choices, so I want to share some insights that may help you.

Remember the parable of the seeds in Matthew 13:3-9? Some seeds were sown on rocky places where the soil had no depth, and because the seeds had no roots, they withered away. The seeds that fell on thorns were choked out. But the seeds that fell on the good soil became fruitful.

Remember, you can choose the soil in which you will be planted. Choose carefully! There are many ways to meet people and make friends. For example, tennis, bridge, golf, social clubs, volunteer work, and jobs are all worthy social outlets. Some women, however, choose to be involved in this social scene to ease the pain of loneliness that comes with moving. It's easy to sink down into busyness and lose yourself in soil that appears to be fertile. Be aware that getting involved in these areas could be like placing yourself in the soil that had no depth and no room for roots. The seed withered away, and so could you. In order for our watered roots to grow deep, we need to be grounded in the nurturing and loving soil of Jesus Christ. Then, all the other things in our lives can grow.

The best way to grow healthy plants is to water them regularly without drenching them, to provide ample light and fertilizer as needed, and to prune the branches when necessary. Here are some ways for you to grow deep roots in the soil of God's love.

Water regularly by staying in God's word! My potted plants are watered daily because they are not in the ground where the sprinkler can reach them. They are separated from the other plants, and can dry out easily. Since your move, you may have become separated from God's word for any number of reasons. Don't dry out! Spend time daily reading the Bible to replenish and restore your soul.

Provide yourself with plenty of light by knowing God's truth. As you read His word, memorize scripture, and believe in His promises, truth will be revealed to you. Tremendous growth will come from allowing God to shine on your life.

Fertilize as needed by being in Christian fellowship. God puts Christian people in your life to nurture you, to serve as models for you, to encourage you, to pray for you, and to hold you accountable. *Seek out a church home, if you haven't already.* Find out if the church has a newcomer's class or support group to help you through your adjustment.

Prune the branches when necessary. Careful pruning allows new growth. Cut away all the old branches and dead flowers. I love to pick withering flowers because the more of them you cut, the more the plant will bloom. The more branches you prune, the fuller and greener the bush becomes.

Gail MacDonald says it best in her book *High Call, High Privilege*.

"Removing the spent blossoms on petunias is essential to new blossoms. Today as I removed the old, I was reminded of how essential it is to my life to enjoy each blossom in my life, but to remember to pull it off when spent and move on to new experiences. Many live trying to keep memories of dead blossoms alive only to miss the potential of the new and present bloom." [1]

"May your roots go down deep into the soil of God's marvelous love" (Eph. 3:17, TLB).

♥   Heart Talk   ♥

Across the long driveway to my grandmother's house grew a magnificent, glorious wisteria vine with long purple flowers that looked like grape clusters. Wisteria vines are strong and sturdy, and usually twine around trees, fences, or porch roofs. This particular one wrapped around a large oak tree. My cousins and I would pull loose one of the vines and swing across the driveway (Tarzan style) from a perch in the old oak tree. We got hours of entertainment out of that old vine.

The memory of that wisteria vine lingers with me even after some 40 years. It carries a special meaning for me the older I get. The vine that wrapped around the oak tree is like God's love wrapped around me. The wisteria vine has become so strong and sturdy with time, that nothing can disentangle it from the oak tree. Similarly, God's love is so strong and sturdy that nothing can separate His love from me.

That wonderful dangling vine that held me as I would swing across the driveway, is much like God's hand. He has carried me across the many miles of my life and throughout all my moves. I pray that you, too, will feel God's loving arms wrapped around you as you make your move!

Bloom From Within

As a mover, you are very much like a daffodil bulb. When planted, you lie dormant for a season until you put down roots. Then your sprout begins to appear above the earth, and finally, you bloom. I suspect that during this move, you've given priority to everyone else in your family, leaving your own sprouts to look pretty wilted. Let's pick off the dead leaves and flowers and give *you* the opportunity to bloom.

Now I want you to put on your sunbonnet, because we're going to have a garden party! I want to celebrate you! As we gather together, you can come as:

Daisy Mover—she mixes well and is usually found in groups
Zinnia Mover—everybody knows her because she's dependable
Forget-me-not Mover—she's so dainty; you won't forget her!
Rose Mover—is so popular with everyone
Petunia Mover—is extremely versatile
Pansy Mover—has a charming and uplifting face
Impatiens Mover—guess you've figured her out!
Azalea Mover—adds permanent value to her surroundings
Begonia Mover—fits in anywhere she lives
Geranium Mover—adds so much color to a group

You see, it takes all kinds of women, as well as all kinds of flowers, to make a beautiful garden. Each one adds its own fragrance, its own uniqueness, and its own beauty. Someone once said, "Who we are is God's gift to us. What we become is our gift to God." At your garden party, I want to help you become your best!

Become your best through the fragrance of your life. "God . . . manifests through us the sweet aroma of the knowledge of Him in every place. For we are a fragrance of Christ to God" (2 Cor. 2:14-15). Have you ever walked through the perfume section of a department store and been drawn to a certain fragrance? When you walk around carrying the aroma of Christ, people will be drawn to you. What will make you different in your community is not that you are new in town, but that the fragrance of Christ surrounds you. You will be known not only by how you bloom, but by His fragrance that you wear.

Become your best through your uniqueness. "For Thou didst form my inward parts; Thou didst weave me in my mother's womb. I will give thanks to Thee, for I am fearfully and wonderfully made" (Psa. 139:13-14). Isn't it great to know you are not made with a cookie cutter? You are an original! That's the very best reason to be yourself, love yourself, and be good to yourself! God made you unique because He wanted your bloom to be one of a kind, distinct from all the others.

Become your best through your beauty. "One thing. . . I shall seek . . . to behold the beauty of the Lord" (Psa. 27:4). Christ is the creator of all beauty, both inside and outside. Your outer beauty is only skin deep. It's the beauty from within that radiates in your life. I would rather see your heart than your hairdo. I'm attracted to what matters to you inside, rather than how you feel about your appearance. It is the indwelling beauty of Christ in your heart that allows your outer beauty to bloom. It takes each person with her own fragrance, uniqueness, and beauty to make a perfect bouquet from the garden. You are, in essence, God's bouquet to the world around you. With that in mind, there are two more things I want you to do at your garden party: celebrate who you are as you bloom from within, and exchange your sunbonnet for a crown.

Need help settling in? In the next chapter, I'll help you make all the "smart moves" with suggestions of things to do, people to see and places to go!

Survival Kit

Thirty Ways to help you "bloom":

1. Eat right.
2. Exercise.
3. Take vitamins.
4. Then treat yourself to a double-dip ice-cream cone!
5. Read that book you always wanted to but never took the time for.
6. Splurge and get a manicure—or a pedicure—or both.
7. Rent an old classic movie that lasts three hours.
8. Go window shopping.
9. Try one new thing each day.
10. Don't compare.
11. Buy yourself pretty stationary to write on.
12. Enjoy a free make-over at a department store.
13. Browse all afternoon in a bookstore.
14. Visit the library. Sit and read your favorite magazines.
15. When you meet someone for the first time, look them in the eyes, and give them a firm handshake and a smile.
16. Focus on being, rather than doing.
17. Seize the day!
18. Buy something wonderful and frivolous for yourself.

19. Expect a positive outcome from your move.
20. Don't feel like you have to be productive all the time.
21. Turn over a new leaf with this move.
22. Pin a fresh flower on your lapel or pocket.
23. Remind yourself it's still okay to cry if you want to.
24. Visit a museum or an art gallery.
25. Treat yourself to a gourmet cup of flavored coffee or exotic herb tea the next time you are at the mall. Enjoy!
26. Take a class in something to expand your interests.
27. Go to a park that has playground equipment and swing!
28. Walk as much as you can.
29. Count your blessings every day.
30. Say your prayers every night.

Chapter 10

The Nitty-Gritty of Getting Settled

I need to focus on how I can get it done,
and not bemoan the fact that I have to do it.
Dianna, a moving friend

After moving to Phoenix from Alabama, Connie said in desperation, "I need all the help I can get! I have so many things to do and so many questions to ask. I don't know where to begin. Can you help me?"

So many times when you move, there isn't anyone around to serve as a resource person for all that needs to be done and learned. If you're like me, and your mind is on overload anyway, all suggestions and ideas are greatly appreciated. That's what this chapter is about—practical suggestions to make your transition easier and to help you settle in.

First of all, remember that you've got a lot going for you as a newcomer in town!

Some of the Advantages of Being New

- You have the chance to start over.
- You will be known for the person you are today, not the person you were yesterday.
- You have more control over your time because you don't have old commitments.
- You have an opportunity to break old labels you've carried.
- You may find time to break old habits.
- You have the opportunity to project a new image.
- Nobody has seen your wardrobe.
- Not only your clothes, but all the things that are old to you, will be new to everyone else.
- You get to experience a new culture.
- You'll have new opportunities for personal and spiritual growth.
- You don't have to meet other people's expectations yet, because they don't have any.
- You'll find new educational and social opportunities.
- Your ideas and perspective will be fresh and new to everyone.
- You have the opportunity to re-prioritize your life.
- Moving will broaden your horizons.
- You'll be able to see God at work in your life.
- Before you get too involved you can find the time to begin, renew, or revitalize your relationship with Jesus Christ.
- You can dwell on all the positive ideas above rather than on the negative things you may hear.

Now your moving friends and I would like to share some of the things that we did to help us get settled.

Twenty-five Things to Do to Help You Get Settled

1. Be prepared to be an initiator!
2. Get a new driver's license.
3. Get new license plates for vehicles.
4. Shop for insurance policies (especially car).
5. Don't forget to look into renter's insurance if you are temporarily or permanently renting.
6. Read the yellow pages to familiarize yourself with services available.

7. Call the Welcome Wagon to visit you.
8. Carry a local map in the car. Use a highlighter to mark places you want to go.
9. Go to the Chamber of Commerce for local information.
10. Get a library card. Check out a book on your new state or city.
11. Subscribe to the local paper. You will learn what's happening, what to do, and also lots of information. For example, when to plant what, how to make local dishes, and what's on sale at the grocery store.
12. Check on places of interest within a day's drive from your city. Great for weekend exploring and entertainment! Take a picnic to the nearest county or state park.
13. Locate the hospital nearest you.
14. A church is a good resource for baby-sitters.
15. Register to vote.
16. Go to the concierge at a local hotel to find out what he or she recommends to do in the area.
17. Find out when garbage pickup is and what recycling procedures your new town has.
18. Find a church home, if you haven't already.
19. Introduce yourself to your mail carrier.
20. Check out banks. Service charges vary. Start checks with the same number your last bank ended with for continuity and merchant reassurance of your stability.
21. It will help you feel established to get "real" mail. Send for things like address labels and free offers to be delivered to your new address.
22. Ask your neighbors to refer you to good service people (plumbers, electricians, etc.).
23. Ask questions. People love to give their opinion and input.
24. Have inexpensive "business cards" printed for identification saying—

THE SMITH FAMILY
BOB, JEAN, BILLY AND BETTY
ADDRESS
PHONE

25. Make a list of emergency numbers:

Ambulance	Pediatrician
Police	Dentist
Fire	Other medical doctors

Security alarm company   Veterinarian
Phone company   Pharmacy
School   Electrician
Work numbers   Plumber
Sitters

Of course, there are many more "to do's" that you've probably already thought of or have already done. Hopefully, these will help you cover some more bases.

Forty Things You Need to Know

1. What are some local customs?
2. What do people do here for leisure or entertainment?
3. What foods are popular here?
4. What department store is most like my favorite back home?
5. Where does the school bus stop?
6. Is my yard used as a cut-through or a shortcut to school?
7. Where are outlets or bargain places located?
8. Where are the bike trails? Jogging trails? Walking trails?
9. What cleaners have one-day service?
10. Do you know a good handyman who will, for example, install ceiling fans?
11. Can you turn right on a red light here?
12. Can you recommend a pest control service?
13. What hairdresser gives the best haircuts?
14. What's the price of a good haircut here?
15. Where's the best restaurant for breakfast?
16. Where's the best place for a "ladies lunch"?
17. Is there a place that serves afternoon tea?
18. Ask any of your favorite restaurant questions?
19. Tell me where *not* to go for child care.
20. Can you recommend any sitters?
21. Is there a florist in town who does unusual arrangements with grapevine baskets, raffia and dried flowers?
22. What are the grocery store chains here?
23. What grocery store has the best meats?
24. Where can I find my favorite regional foods? (Grits!)
25. Tell me about the churches in the area.

26. Is there a "neighborhood watch" here?
27. What major companies are based here?
28. What's the main source of income for the city? (tourism, farming, etc.)
29. Is there a Christian radio station here?
30. What kind of public transportation does the city have?
31. Are there areas of town that we should avoid?
32. Are there places or areas I should tell my teenager are not safe?
33. Can you recommend a car mechanic? Is there one I should stay away from?
34. Where's the best place to work out? Are there any aerobics classes?
35. Are there any ordinances or neighborhood covenants I need to be aware of? (No parking on street, etc.)
36. Where is a place to get my nails done?
37. Do you know a housekeeper? What's the going rate?
38. Who is a decorator? Have you seen his or her work?
39. What are the free local events and activities?
40. What is one thing you think I need to know as a newcomer?

♥   Heart Talk   ♥

A little tip from me to you—don't try to ask all these questions in one day! Just be ready to ask, when the opportunity arises, about those things that will shape your lifestyle for the next few years. I suggest that you make a list of questions you want to ask. Get input on what your husband and children need and want to know. Always share what you learn with your family. Remember, they also need help in making the transition to a new place.

Make the most of all the opportunities available to you, whether you are in a city or a small town. Greet people with a smile and a positive attitude! Remember that each person you meet is a potential friend!

Did you know that loneliness and loss of identity are the two leading responses from newcomers when they are asked, "What was the hardest thing about your move?" In the next two chapters, we'll talk about both of these issues!

Chapter 11

A Place in Your Heart
Called Loneliness

I will never desert you, nor will I ever forsake you.
Hebrews 13:5

Their dream had come true. Julie's husband had been accepted at graduate school. They were young, ready for new challenges, and eager for the opportunity to be near Julie's family on the West Coast. Everything had fallen into place just as they had planned, and they looked forward to this move.

They found a small cottage to rent near campus, and Julie got a teaching job. But soon, after the newness wore off, loneliness set in. Julie began to dislike everything about the new place where they lived. She had come from a small town in South Carolina to a big city in California. She felt isolated and lonely.

"Everyone is so busy," she said with discouragement in her voice. "It's so hard to get close to people. I feel like there isn't anyone who really knows me, or anyone I really know. The hardest thing about moving is being alone and not having a good friend to call and talk to. My husband and I are very close, but feeling so alone has caused conflict between us at times. I miss having a close friend."

Six months after they moved, Elaine felt good about supporting her husband in his ministry and working with him as a team. But she also felt very lonely and hurt. "I had left behind my coworkers and friends and had no one to talk to. I felt hurt, because it seemed like people here didn't come up to me and talk. I had to be the one to initiate the conversation."

A year later she was still feeling lonely. "I guess because I'm a pastor's wife, I just can't talk to people the way I could if I were not," Elaine said. "It's hard to find someone I can trust and with whom I can share my thoughts and fears."

Melinda's loneliness from moving was bad enough, but it was compounded when her husband started traveling immediately after their move. He was usually gone Monday through Friday. She was shy, quiet, and not an initiator. "I feel like I'm on the outside of a sliding glass door looking in, and nobody stops to open the door and ask me if I want to come in," Melinda said as she gazed off into the distance. Besides everything else, the couple's children were grown and married. "The loneliness in my heart is unbearable," Melinda confessed.

Julie, Elaine, and Melinda have all felt the pain of loneliness and isolation that comes as a result of moving. Their stories are not unique. Because one in five Americans moves each year, the feelings of loneliness and being disconnected from friends, family, and community affect millions of women every day.

Vance Packard says in his book *A Nation of Strangers*,

"We are seeing a sharp increase of people suffering alienation or just feeling adrift, which is having an impact on emotional and even physical health. We know there is a substantial increase of inhabitants suffering a sense of loss of community, identity, and continuity. These losses all contribute to a deteriorating sense of well-being, both for individuals and for society. In all this disruption of familiar patterns, some people respond with a deepened sense of loneliness."[1]

Many of us live in houses where we enter by pushing a button on the garage door opener. The garage door opens, we drive in, then push the button again to close the door behind us. Our yards have six-foot-high privacy fences or concrete walls, preventing us from connecting with our neighbors. Any social contact happens not by coincidence, but by effort. My friend Sudie used to laugh and say, "When you first move, the only one who knows you by name is 'Tilly the Teller,' the automatic banking machine!" Another moving friend said that she looked forward to a wrong number call or someone calling to sell something, just to hear the phone ring!

According to Webster's Dictionary, loneliness is the feeling of being "isolated; unhappy at being alone; longing for friends." Another definition I read said that loneliness is the emotional pain caused by social or emotional isolation from intimate relationships. Our mobile society has certainly contributed to the loneliness of millions of people.

Gilligan's Island

Have you ever felt like one of the castaways on Gilligan's Island, isolated from the rest of the world? In Ben Ferguson's book, *God I've got a Problem*,[2] he relates loneliness to that popular television series from the '70s. It depicts a group of people marooned on an island, frantically sending distress signals to the outside world. I can remember watching Gilligan and his crew frantically waving to passing ships in the hope that someone would rescue them from their plight.

At times you've probably felt that no one saw your frantic distress signals as they passed by your island of loneliness. You were left alone without anyone slowing down or looking your way. All you could do was hope that eventually someone would see you or hear your cry.

In a Whisper

A newcomer to Phoenix, Judy told me her story of how she had been rescued from her island of loneliness.

"The second day we moved here," Judy said, "I was running errands in a borrowed car. It was a typical August afternoon in Phoenix, with the temperature over 110 degrees. We had sold both of our cars in Maryland and had borrowed a car until we could buy one. The borrowed car had a lot of broken gauges, and the windows and wipers didn't work, but the air conditioner was cold, so I was fine.

"While I was out gathering things to set up the house, the car stalled in a major intersection. I didn't have any idea where to get help and knew no one to call. My husband couldn't come get me, because we had only that one car. Finally, some people stopped and pushed my car out of the intersection and into the shade near a gas station. They could see I was really frazzled. I walked over to the station and got some gas, hoping it was only a broken gas gauge."

"I contained my tears until I got home, but then went to my room to yell and sob my anger and frustration at God (no use yelling at my husband or kids). 'How could You send me here? I can't find anything. I can't even find a gas station!' I ranted and raved for awhile. After I cried myself out, I just kept repeating, 'I can't find anything, I can't find anything,' until I heard that still, small voice of God say to me, 'You can always find Me.' I knew in my heart that was what really mattered. Christ is with me everywhere I go. I'm never really alone. He didn't tell me I would always be happy, but He did promise He would always be with me!"

As Judy cried out in distress, God reassured her of His presence. She felt His comfort easing the ache of loneliness in her heart. Something else of great significance happened as well. Even in the midst of feeling the pain of loneliness, Judy was listening for God! He spoke to her in a whisper, and if she had not been listening, she would never have heard His reassurance and encouragement.

Think about Elijah, one of the great men in the Bible. There was a time in his life when he, too, felt overwhelmed by loneliness and fear.

"Go out and stand before Me on the mountain," the Lord told him. As Elijah stood there, the Lord passed by, and a mighty windstorm hit the mountain, but the Lord was not in the wind. After the wind, there was an earthquake, but the Lord was not in the earthquake. And after the earthquake, there was a fire, but the Lord was not in the fire. And after the fire, there was the sound of a gentle whisper (1 Kings 19:11-12, TLB). That's when the Lord spoke to Elijah.

God didn't speak through the spectacular things that were happening. He spoke in the quietness of a still, small voice—a gentle whisper. "Be still and know that I am God" (Psa. 46:10, KJV).

♥   Heart Talk   ♥

Are you listening for God's voice? What is He whispering to you in your loneliness? Could He be saying, "Come closer to Me, so you can hear Me"?

How can you hear God speak if you are isolated from Him or if you have chosen to be separated from Him? "Draw near to God and He will draw near to you" (James 4:8). My prayer for you at this very moment is that the loneliness you feel from this move will become the vehicle that drives you to Jesus Christ. I want you to have the pleasure of His company in your loneliness.

Have you ever felt isolated in a room full of people, in a long, dark hospital corridor, at a party, at a Bible study, in a beautiful new home, as a newcomer, in the midst of friends, and perhaps even in church? I have, and I know the pain of feeling disconnected from everyone. I've felt the emptiness that aches inside and the isolation that leaves one numb. I've been lonely, but I've never been alone. My relationship with Christ and His presence in my life sustains me. I have the pleasure of His company.

What I've Learned About Loneliness

In Tim Hansel's book *Through the Wilderness of Loneliness*, he expresses so beautifully what loneliness is.

> "Loneliness is not a time of abandonment . . . it just feels that way. It's actually a time of encounter at new levels with the only One who can fill that empty place in our hearts. Loneliness need not be an enemy . . . it can be a friend. Loneliness need not be an interruption in our lives. . . . it can be a gift. Loneliness need not be an obstacle . . . it can be an invitation. Loneliness need not be a problem . . . it can be an opportunity. Loneliness need not be a dead end . . . it can be an adventure!" [3]

If we were sitting together in my hammock once more, I would share with you some of the things I've learned about loneliness.

Feel the pain. Remember your luggage tags in chapter 7? Loneliness may be one of the tags you are wearing. It may be the hardest thing you are dealing with in your move. Don't stuff it, don't deny it—if you can't feel it, you can't heal it! Jesus knows about loneliness. He felt its pain when He went to the Garden of Gethsemane to pray. Jesus asked three of His disciples, "Stay here and watch with Me." When He returned from praying, He found His three closest friends sound asleep. How lonely and abandoned He must have felt. "Could you not keep watch for one hour?" He said. Three times He went off to pray, and three times His disciples abandoned Him for sleep (Mark 14:32-40). Jesus can comfort you through your pain, because He has felt the emotion of loneliness.

C.S. Lewis said that God whispers to us in our joys and shouts to us in our pain. God may be using this move and the pain of your loneliness to get your full attention and draw you closer to Him.

Listen. Shhh! What is God trying to tell you?

- That He wants to reassure you of His love. "I have loved you with an everlasting love" (Jer. 31:3).
- That He wants to encourage you with His presence. "I will be with you; I will not fail you or forsake you" (Josh. 1:5).
- That He has moved you here for a reason and a purpose, and you are to trust Him completely. "Trust in the Lord with all your heart, and do not lean on your own understanding" (Prov. 3:5).

There have been many times when loneliness overwhelmed me, and I was so busy interpreting all the events of my life that I didn't hear what God was saying about the situation. May we never forget—when God takes the time to speak to us, we need to listen.

Focus on Christ. Don't try to fill up your life with people, things, or activities to escape from loneliness. The emptiness you feel should first be filled by God; then He will bring the right people into your life to ease the loneliness.

Augustine said that there is a God-shaped vacuum in all of us that only He can fill. How can you fill that vacuum with God? Take this "down time" in your life and get to know Him intimately through Bible study and prayer. Build a relationship with Him. Then, you will come out the other side of loneliness a stronger and more confidently fulfilled woman. "As a deer pants for the water brooks, so my soul pants for Thee, O God. My soul thirsts for God, for the living God" (Psa. 42:1-2).

Rest in Him. I have often thought that the only time I'm not too busy, too scheduled, and committed over my head is right after I move! For many of us, that pocket of time is like a clock that's waiting to be wound. Until our life starts ticking again, we have a time of rest and we often waste it by being frantic about our loneliness.

I'm a people person and my effectiveness in giving and doing things for others is in direct proportion to the rest, solitude, and quiet time I spend with my Lord. I learned this lesson the hard way.

There was a time when I poured myself out to others without first being filled up through spending time with God. It didn't work and I ended up running on empty! Take the pocket of time God has given you and rest from your busyness. Spend quiet time with Jesus. His arms are big enough to hold you for as long as you need His comfort. "Come to Me, all who are weary and heavy-laden, and I will give you rest," He says (Matt. 11:28).

God is your refuge. Think about David—one of my favorite people in the Bible. He ran to God a lot. Talk about somebody that feels his pain! David loved God, questioned God, and was angry at God. He was happy, sad, joyful, depressed, and lonely. But he knew where to go to retreat! "God is our refuge and strength, a very present help in trouble" (Psa. 46:1).

Peace. When you accept your circumstances and feel contentment, then peace will follow. It's when you fight, kick, and rebel against your circumstances, and allow loneliness to have a negative effect on every part of your life, that your spirit will be in turmoil, lacking peace. Remember, God doesn't always take your loneliness away, but rather uses it in your life to make you stronger. You can have peace in the midst of loneliness—a peace that comes only from knowing God.

The apostle Paul knew this peace. He suffered the anguish of loneliness in prison. Instead of feeling sorry for himself though, he studied and prepared for the day he would be released (2 Tim. 4:13).

Paul learned "the secret of being content in any and every situation" (Phil. 4:12, NIV). You can learn that secret too. "Peace I leave with you; My peace I give to you" (Jn. 14:27).

Reach Out. Are you waiting for others to reach out to you? Many times after a move, I've dreamed of neighbors knocking on my door to welcome me into the neighborhood and to bring me flowers, a fresh-baked pie or brownies, a list of places to go and things to do. You know, like Ozzie and Harriet would do in a minute! For all the times people have reached out to me, there have been just as many times they haven't. I can choose to feel sorry for myself and indulge in a lot of self-pity. But that's not the answer. The answer is to stop thinking about me, and start thinking about thee!

Joan, a moving friend, offered good advice for newcomers. She said, "Reach out to others. There are plenty of people more needy than we are." Who knows, they could even be your neighbors. So, I have learned to pursue others, to make it happen, to jump in, to just do it! That's not easy for shy women to do, but it's one of the conditions of being "a mover." You've just gotta grit your teeth and do it!

One of the joys in my life has been to see newcomers reaching out to other newcomers in our church. That's what's so wonderful about having a newcomers' class. The members reach out and minister to each other. I have often seen them hug, take meals to one another, hold hands and pray together, grieve together, grow together in Christ, take care of each other's children, cry together, visit each other in the hospital, financially help each other, laugh together, and heal together! "Do for others what you want them to do for you" (Matt. 7:12, TLB).

In Elisabeth Elliot's wonderful book *Loneliness*, she says,

> "The answer to our loneliness is love—not our finding someone to love us, but our surrendering to the God who has always loved us with an everlasting love. Loving Him is then expressed in a happy and full-hearted pouring out of ourselves in love to others."[4]

These are the things I want to share with you as we sit in my hammock. Tuck them in your heart. Tuck them into the place called loneliness, and remember that God has not forgotten you.

According to the responses to my questionnaire, the second hardest thing about moving is loss of identity! A moving friend told me once that she had moved so many times she didn't know *where* she was, much less *who* she was! So, in the next chapter, let's find out who you really are.

Survival Kit

This chapter dealt mostly with actions you take in your heart. Now let's balance the inward actions with some outward activities that will help alleviate loneliness:

- One moving friend wrote that she sold Avon when she moved to a new place. It helped her meet people quickly!
- Another had all the contractors (and their wives) who built her new home over for an appreciation dinner!
- Hit the garage sales on Friday and Saturday mornings. You can learn your way around your new town and have fun doing it.
- Find a Christian bookstore in town. Just being there will give you a warm feeling inside.
- Sign up to be "greeters" at church.
- Volunteer your home for school meetings, neighborhood meetings and church meetings.
- Join "Moms in Touch."

- Volunteer to collect for United Way, Cancer Drive or any community fund-raiser in your neighborhood.
- Have a neighborhood coffee yourself! Put invitations in everybody's mailbox.
- Don't feel sorry for yourself.
- Remember, "This too shall pass."

Chapter 12

Nobody Knows My Name

"Who are you?" said the caterpillar.
"I—I hardly know, Sir, just at present," Alice replied rather shyly.
"At least I know who I was when I got up this morning, but I think
I must have been changed several times since then."
Lewis Carroll—*Alice's Adventures in Wonderland*

I kept Marian's letter in my treasure box for several years. She lived in Phoenix some time back and has since moved away. Her letter expresses what so many of you have told me over and over again!

"Tears come as I think back to the first year of transition here in this new town," Marian wrote. "I made so many sacrifices in this move, but the greatest was my immediate and devastating loss of identity. Here I was, in the midst of the desert with nothing—truly nothing. I had been stripped of the roles I had played: wife of the successful corporate executive, keeper of the lovely home, busy and involved mom of four, and loyal friend with meaningful relationships. Plus, I didn't even know how to get to the grocery store or anywhere else I needed to go."

Marian's letter echoed the banner that all movers painfully hold up, "Fragile—Identity Lost in Move."

Lost—My Credentials

I shared with you earlier how the biggest luggage tag I wore in moving was one that read "LOSS OF IDENTITY." That was the most difficult obstacle I had to face in my effort to start over. I really felt as if I'd lost my credentials and nobody knew my name! I wanted to wear a sign around my neck saying, "My name is . . . This is what I can do . . . I really am a nice person to know and I'd love to talk to you!" It may sound silly, but I was desperate! As a newcomer, I didn't have any history in this place. It was as if I had to identify myself all over again. I had a basic need to be accepted and loved in my new world, and yet nobody knew me well enough to accept me or to love me. I wanted instant results, but love and acceptance take time. I wanted to belong somewhere, so I tried to fit in by being someone I wasn't. I felt inadequate in my new surroundings. I sank further into despair as my self-esteem dropped lower and lower. I asked myself, *What's happening to me? Where is that confident person I once was? What happened to the person who knew who she was and felt like she had it all together? Why can't I get a grip on life?*

I prayed for the strength to overcome my feelings. I cried out to God to help me rise above the emotions. But God had me right where He wanted me—in a place of total dependence on Him. God wanted me to start over and He brought me to the desert so He could be the only one to quench my thirst. He was my only oasis. My emotional survival was dependent on Him alone.

The loss of identity I felt in moving is echoed in the voices of movers everywhere. Alma comments on her move from Colorado to Arizona, "I was pushed out of my comfort zone, and I didn't know who I was or how to act. What was my role? I had lost my identity."

Alma had seen herself as a Ph.D. student. She had not yet completed her program when they moved to Phoenix, and when she couldn't continue her studies, she felt a loss of identity. But the good news is that Alma says the move was exactly what her spiritual life cried out for! The Lord led her and her husband to a wonderful church where they started to grow, and they haven't stopped growing since. They have learned to depend on God more and more as He provides for them and meets their needs.

Julie, whom we met in the last chapter, said after her move from the deep South to California, "I felt like a social outcast. No one knew me or talked to me. I kept thinking that something must be wrong with me or people would like me."

The good news is that Julie recently told me that God gave her the courage to meet people, to call them if they didn't call her, and if no one was available, to be content going places alone. She said, "I just kept forcing myself reach out to others, even though I felt so rejected."

Allicia moved to Florida and nearly drowned in her self-pity. She said, "Being new, you always feel like you have to 'sell yourself.' Other people have to make room in their lives for you. I would ask myself, 'Am I worthy enough for them to make room for me?'" The good news about Allicia's story is that God profoundly changed her life. His word spoke to her heart, and Allicia came to know Jesus Christ. Self-pity fled, and as the result of much prayer, contentment came to live in its place.

Judy moved from her hometown in Maryland. She didn't hesitate when she replied, "Every time I move, I have an identity crisis. I question, *Will people like me?* I wonder what to reveal about myself and what to hide. I'm often guarded, edgy about what I say or don't say. I'm uncomfortable with having to explain myself over and over because people don't know my history." Judy's good news is that, "This move, I've made a conscious effort to learn how God meets all my needs. I don't want to be dependent on my husband, on other people, or on things to meet my needs. When I'm lonely, I talk to Christ. When I'm frustrated, I talk to Christ. When I need a friend to share my disorientation, I talk to Christ. Who better than Christ would know what it's like to leave great fellowship and a home He loves, to come to a new strange, new place? I wonder if Christ ever got homesick for heaven?"

When Sudie moved to California—her 10th move—she said, "I feel like I have to prove to people that I'm a neat person. I have to start building my self-confidence all over again. I'm back at square one." Sudie's good news is that she wrote me and said, "I reminded myself that God didn't bring us here to go backward. So many of the pieces still haven't fallen into place, but God has my complete attention! I'm spending more time in prayer than I was. I'm convinced that He's doing something that couldn't have happened in my comfort zone."

These movers may have lost their credentials, but they found their identity—in Christ. Do you feel that you've lost your credentials? Your self-esteem? Let's take a further look in all the right places, not only to find your credentials, but your true identity.

Hey, Look Me Over! What Do You See?

Mirror, mirror on the wall, who's the most insecure of all? Sometimes I dread those three-way mirrors in department stores. They can plunge me into reality more quickly than anything. They tell me far more than I want to know. Not only can I see myself from head to toe, but I can see side and back views! Nothing is hidden; it's all staring back at me—especially when I'm trying on bathing suits! Talk about loss of identity! Any thoughts I may have had about my body looking like those magazine ads are proven to be illusions when I look in that mirror! (I know you're smiling, because you've looked in that same mirror, haven't you?)

Let's step in front of an imaginary *three-way mirror* to look at ourselves physically, spiritually, and emotionally.

Physically. Have you put on a few pounds since the move? Do you need a new hair style? Do your clothes fit the style and the climate of your new area?

Spiritually. Take a look at your relationship with God since you moved. Are you angry at Him? Do you feel close to Him, or are you estranged from Him? Do you really even know who God is?

Emotionally. Do you feel like you're stuck, or are you making progress? Have you worked through any feelings you've struggled with? Are you withdrawn or outgoing?

Then there's the *full-length mirror* I have at home. It gives me a quick overview. It tells me if I'm coordinated, if I'm all together, and if I think I'll make a good first impression. But a full-length mirror only tells us how we look on the outside. We need to take a full-length look inside to see if we are becoming the person God meant us to be. When was the last time you took a good long look at your heart?

A *magnifying mirror* may be small, but it shows everything in a BIG way. A magnifying mirror gives us a closer look at who we are. It allows us to see our blemishes so that we know what action to take to correct them. It gives us a really close look at what needs to be improved and what changes need to be made in our attitude or our outlook. It's wise to take a magnified look at ourselves.

Oh, yes, and I shouldn't forget the *distorted mirror*—the one I look into for fun at the circus or the fair. I always laugh when I see myself in a distorted mirror. At times we all have a distorted view of ourselves, especially when we are trying to be someone we're not. It's hard to see the real person we are when we base our image on false, negative perceptions.

The *best mirror* of all is the one that reflects how God sees us, not how we see ourselves! If you have accepted Jesus as your Lord and Savior, the mirror will show a person who has been cleansed by God's forgiveness! The next time you look in a mirror, imagine that Jesus is standing by your side, looking in the mirror with you. He is smiling, for "you are precious in His sight" (Isa. 43:4), and He loves you more than life itself (1 Jn. 3:16). He sees you with eyes of acceptance (Rom. 15:7), and He values you with all His heart (Matt.10:31). Through Him, you are forgiven (Neh. 9:17). You have no blemishes, no ugliness, no imperfections—only your cleansed heart is visible. Take time to look in this mirror every day!

Found—My Identity

Our true identity is found in Christ, not (as the world would have us believe) in our appearance, our performance, or our status. We can't find our identity through other people. God wants to be the most significant person in our lives. He wants us to know that, in Christ, we are always accepted.

In Dr. Bill Yarger's tapes *A Biblical View of You*, he shares that our security, significance, and strength can only be met through Christ:

"Our security is in knowing we are loved totally and unconditionally (Jer. 31:3). We cannot be any more loved by God than we are. He gave His only Son to die for us. No one can add to or take away from that.

Our significance lies in being aware of our personal value and meaning (Jer. 29:11-13). We are God's representatives—invaluable creatures!

Our strength comes when we realize our spiritual resources and the God-given competence to overcome our circumstances (Phil. 4:13). Because of God's presence in our lives, we simply can't be more adequate than we already are." [1]

We all have a need to feel loved and accepted. We all need to feel like we belong somewhere or to someone. If these things are lacking, or are out of balance because of our move, it can contribute to our loss of identity, self-esteem, or self-image. That's why it's so vital for us to know who we are in Christ. What a security it is to know we belong to Him, that He loves us and accepts us no matter who we are or where we are!

I've found my identity, have you?

Who you are in Christ.

Jesus wants you to know that you are most precious to Him.

"The Lord your God has chosen you...to be His people, His treasured possession" (Deut. 7:6, NIV).

You are incredibly loved!

"I have loved you with an everlasting love" (Jer. 31:3).

You are known inside and out!

"O Lord, Thou hast searched me and known me" (Psa. 139:1).

You are accepted with no strings attached!

"He hath made us accepted in the beloved" (Eph. 1:6, KJV).

You are in process to become like Christ!

"For I am confident of this very thing, that He who began a good work in you will perfect it until the day of Christ Jesus" (Phil. 1:6).

You are valued beyond measure!

"See how great a love the Father has bestowed upon us, that we should be called children of God" (1 Jn. 3:1).

You are custom-designed and unique!

"For Thou didst form my inward parts; Thou didst weave me in my mother's womb . . . I am fearfully and wonderfully made" (Psa. 139:13-14).

You are made for a reason and a purpose!

"Before I formed you in the womb I knew you, and before you were born I consecrated you" (Jer. 1:5).

There is someone who knows your name!

"Do not fear, for I have redeemed you; I have called you by name; you are Mine!" (Isa. 43:1)

♥　Heart Talk　♥

May we have a heart talk? It doesn't matter how many mirrors you look into, my friend. Until you take off your mask, you can't see who you really are. Some of you have hidden behind a mask because it protects you from the anguish of a troubled marriage or a broken relationship. It could be a safe place to hide where you don't have to face the pain and heartache in your life. Maybe it's a cover-up for your loss of identity, your damaged self-image, or your fragile self-esteem. Whatever the reason, I'm giving you permission to take off your mask now! Don't you see? When you have a God who loves you unconditionally, accepts you just as you are, values you above all else, knows everything about you, and will never ever leave you, it's okay to be the real you! And a great time to become real is when you're starting over in a new place.

There's a wonderful freedom in taking off your mask and letting God's love shine on your face and heart, warming you. I know, because I took off my mask, and if I can do it, so can you!

Margery Williams' charming book *The Velveteen Rabbit* contains this exchange:

> "What is REAL?" asked the Rabbit.
>
> "Real isn't how you are made," said the Skin Horse. "It's a thing that happens to you. When a child loves you for a long, long time, not just to play with, but REALLY loves you, then you become Real."
>
> "Does it hurt?" asked the Rabbit.
>
> "Sometimes," said the Skin Horse, for he was always truthful. "When you are Real, you don't mind being hurt."[2]

God has loved you for a long, long time—REALLY loved you.

Now *you* can become real as well.

Remember Marian's letter at the beginning of this chapter? This is how she ended it, "The loss of identity that crushed me is gradually reshaping me into the likeness of my dear Jesus."

In the next three chapters we'll talk about some subjects that are near and dear to our hearts—our husbands, our children, and our friends. What do a cake mix and a husband have in common? Read on.

Chapter 13

Have I Told You Lately That I Love You?

For where you go, I will go, and where you lodge, I will lodge.
Ruth 1:16

Have you asked yourself, "How is this move affecting my marriage?" Teri, a newcomer did, and this is what she shared with me about her marriage and move.

"Our move created an emotional distance between my husband and me. We were separated for three months while I stayed behind to sell the house and wait for the children to get out of school. We both got used to functioning independently. Neither of us felt we needed the other the way we had before the move. It took a couple of months for us to even begin to feel as if were functioning as a couple and as a family again."

Teri is not alone in her feelings about her husband and their move. When I asked other newcomers how moving had affected their marriage, they were eager to share both the positive and the negative. Here are some of their comments.

"We have always been extremely close, but we have had to weather conflict caused by my loneliness. He had to be everything for me."

"He became consumed with his work and I felt left out."

"Overall, I'd say it made us closer. At first, all we had was each other for companionship."

"Because of the instability of his new job, we drew closer together. Even though there was change all around us, our relationship was constant. We hadn't changed and that familiarity felt good."

"The move created conflict at first, because I'd left a lot behind, but then the move brought us closer because we only had each other. Since my schedule had come to a standstill, I had more time to give, and less stress."

"We have been on an emotional roller coaster with six jobs in three years. It's been too many adjustments and has created a lot of problems."

"I felt resentful that nothing seemed to ruffle him."

"When I'm feeling sorry for myself, it's easy for me to blame my husband for my difficult circumstances. If I can see the situation with a sense of humor, it helps everything."

Don't overlook the effects that moving can have on your marriage! The changes and adjustments that come with your transition are only natural. For many women, those changes and adjustments bring their marriage relationship closer; for others it's just another brick in the wall between them. It is my hope that through this chapter, you will seize the opportunity to make this move a move closer to each other, and that you will develop a deeper understanding and sensitivity to your husband.

My Moving Man

When Bill and I were dating, I remember telling him in a romantic voice, "I'll follow you to the ends of the earth!" Fourteen moves and 30 years of marriage later, I still would! When Bill chose the hotel business as a career, it seemed the address at our house would always be changing. Since hotels are open 24 hours a day, 365 days a year, and their busiest restaurant times are holidays, guess who was left alone a lot? There were times when I felt, *Even the Lone Ranger has Tonto—and all I have is empty boxes!* Needless to say, our "marriage on the move" has gone through every phase and stage, every feeling and emotion—from heartache to happiness.

Don't Forget to Unpack Your Husband

I must admit there have been times when I wanted to pack Bill in a box and store him in the garage! And there have been times when I've been insensitive to his needs and emotions, and have forgotten to unpack him in the move!

In order to help you unpack your husband carefully, you've got to understand your man. I've come up with four different types of husbands who move, based on my observations and what women who have moved told me.

Working Willy
- another name for workaholic
- a great provider
- goes to work early and works late
- works on weekends
- never knows when he's going to be home for dinner
- has little time left over for wife and children
- is climbing the corporate ladder—thrives on promotions
- will move every two to three years if necessary
- is excited to move—gets recognition and fits right in

Working Willy appears to:
- be a high achiever
- seek to gain value through performance
- be a driven person
- have a deep need for approval

Jock O' Jerry
- his life is centered around golf, tennis, racquetball, or some other sport
- extra time goes to developing work and social relationships. Tennis and golf tee times are on Saturday and Sunday mornings—no time for church involvement
- doesn't have a serious side—a big joker
- adapts to the role of being one of the children, rather than the parent
- he's moving to a new playground full of friends—new competition
- checks out all sports available in area before moving
- centers conversation around sports, jobs, and politics
- superficial

Jock O'Jerry appears to:
- be insecure
- be afraid to feel anything beneath the surface
- put on a front so no one can get inside
- have a deep need to be accepted
- be fearful of rejection

Serious Sam
- driven by an inner need to conquer life
- inquisitive—has to understand everything
- spends time reading computer manuals
- buys the latest computer programs
- difficult to reach—guarded
- unemotional—introverted
- will do an-in depth study of every aspect of the move beforehand
- will see all the negatives about moving before the positives
- cautious

  Serious Sam appears to:
- be filled with pride
- be someone who is afraid of being wrong
- lack confidence
- be fearful of being known
- be afraid of rejection

Unaware Harry
- dedicated to family
- puts children first
- doesn't connect with real needs of his wife
- in his eyes he's done the best he can
- well thought of by everyone around him
- thinks that by providing physical comforts his wife is happy
- believes when he moves the family, it will be a wonderful experience for everyone

  Unaware Harry appears to:
- be just that—unaware
- be in need of guidance
- be in need of a mentor-role model
- be insensitive

You may identify some of these characteristics in your husband, or you may find that none of them apply to him. The main thing is to zero in on the type of "moving man" you have so that you can better understand him. What do you do then?

- Pray about it. Remember you can't change your husband, but God can!
- Identify your feelings. Are you angry, hurt, resentful?
- Communicate your feelings. Remember it's not what you say, but how you say it. Pray about that too.
- Love him unconditionally. No strings attached. Show it with your eyes, your smile, your touch.
- Accept him totally for what he is, not for what you want him to be.
- Be ready to forgive him. With forgiveness, healing can begin.

In the course of our marriage, by his own admission, Bill has been several of these types. He's been Working Willy—where do you think I got the name? Unaware Harry, and he claimed a few of the other characteristics too.

I loved him then, and I love him now. Over the years, God has worked in both our lives to bring us to the place where we are today in our marriage. At the bottom of a picture taken of Bill and me some years ago, is this verse, "Now to Him who is able to do exceeding abundantly beyond all that we ask or think, according to the power that works within us, to Him be the glory!" (Eph. 3:20-21)

I claimed that verse for our marriage. I readily admit that it has been Christ who has empowered our marriage far beyond all that I could ever ask or think.

What Do Your Husband and a Cake Mix Have in Common?

They both come with basic ingredients and usually there's something you have to add to the mix! When you buy a cake mix at the store it is a mixture of flour, sugar, corn starch, and baking soda. You add water, eggs, and oil. Sometimes there's pudding in the mix, sometimes you have to add other ingredients yourself. Then, to complete the cake, you bake it, cool it, and frost it.

When you get married, your husband comes packaged with his own basic genetic characteristics, environmental background, and family influences. You add the extra ingredients of acceptance, affirmation, encouragement, praise, and value. Sometimes his self-esteem is strong, sometimes you have to encourage it. Then you add the frosting—love! (Bet you'll think about your husband the next time you bake a cake!)

All of the extra things you add to the mix not only help you encourage your husband after a move; they are also the ingredients which can give your marriage a new beginning!

Back to Basics

Don't neglect spending time in God's word. It will give you the boost you need for your new beginning.

"Let the wife see that she respects *and* reverences her husband— that she notices him, regards him, honors him, prefers him, venerates and esteems him; and that she defers to him, praises him, and loves and admires him exceedingly" (Eph. 5:33, TAB).

"Let no unwholesome word proceed from your mouth, but only such a word as is good for edification according to the need of the moment" (Eph. 4:29).

"Not that we are adequate in ourselves to consider anything as *coming* from ourselves, but our adequacy is from God" (2 Cor. 3:5).

"And let us not lose heart in doing good, for in due time we shall reap if we do not grow weary" (Gal. 6:9).

"Let all bitterness and wrath and anger and clamor and slander be put away from you, along with all malice. And be kind to one another, tender-hearted, forgiving each other, just as God in Christ also has forgiven you" (Eph. 4:31-32).

♥   Heart Talk   ♥

I want you to think back to the time when you fell in love with your husband. You chose him and committed your heart to him. The fact that you loved him made your life wonderful. Every day with him was special. You would wear your best Sunday dress and your Sunday smile just for him. Then somewhere along the way, you became disappointed and disillusioned with him. The Sundays became weekdays and you began to wear only your everyday clothes. You were Cinderella-minded back then. You remembered only the part about "living happily ever after." You forgot that before the story came to a wonderful ending, Cinderella experienced sorrow and hardship, disillusionment and disappointment. In real life, those struggles often continue on and on, making you think there won't ever be a happy ending.

Life is not always easy. But you can choose to love your husband again, to trust your heart to him again, and to find those special days to wear your Sunday dress and smile again. Then you can whisper in his ear, "Have I told you lately that I love you?"

A Letter from Don

I received this letter from the husband of a dear friend in Colorado. He wanted you to know some ways in which his wife encouraged him through the moving process. It offers great insight from a man's perspective:

Marian encouraged me by her selfless giving to God's greater purpose, and by unconditionally giving of herself to our children and to me. She is a model mom. Through her gifts of wisdom and organization, she provides the priorities and focus for our family. She accepts her position as Mom by insuring that our children are growing spiritually, settled in school, provided for at church, and comforted at home. The trauma of moving is looked at nose-to-nose and dealt with. Knowing that our children are more than surviving gives me confidence and assurance. She watches me and lovingly points out when I'm distracted by work, grumpy with the kids, and neglecting our family.

She is a lighthouse, always helping me stay on course. She rebukes me when I sometimes long to be back in Arizona. She instills an eagerness in each of us to look for the blessing in each situation. She listens and talks through the anguish of new job adjustments. We recognize the difficulties, talk about them, deal with them—and then move on to more fruitful and pleasant times.

She talks about her own hopes and dreams. By having the wisdom of discernment, Marian can recognize and define hopes and opportunities. And, of course, all of this is possible because of her commitment and loving relationship to Jesus.

She seeks. She prays. The pain, and the remembrance of the pain of moving is sometimes wrenching. The blessing of new friends, new experiences, new learning, new opportunity is here; but we must reach out and take it. Marian is helping us do that.

Sincerely,

Don

Survival Kit

Twenty-five ways to convey your love:

1. Be his cheerleader—not his critic.
2. Greet him at the door when he comes home from work.
3. Bake his favorite pie.
4. Write a love note and put it in his briefcase or coat pocket.
5. Frame a recent picture of yourself for his office.
6. Hold hands in public or at the movies.
7. Tell him you believe in him.
8. Listen to him.
9. Learn as much as you can about his work.
10. Always kiss him good-bye in the morning.
11. Always kiss him good-night.
12. Call him at work and tell him you are thinking about him.
13. When he returns home from a trip, put a "welcome home" sign on the door.
14. Buy his favorite ice cream.
15. Mail a romantic card to him at his office.
16. Watch a TV sports program with him.
17. Never criticize him in public and never compare him to someone else's husband.
18. Tell him you love him at least once a day.
19. A hug can speak volumes; so can a kiss.
20. Write "I love you" on the bathroom mirror with lipstick.
21. Plan a "date night" and go to his favorite restaurant.
22. Speak of his good qualities; pray about his bad qualities.
23. Anticipate his needs.
24. Look him in the eyes and say, "I'd follow you to the end of the earth."
25. Tell him five reasons you would move anywhere with him.

How do you help your children adjust in a move? Lots of ideas to help you are coming up next!

Chapter 14

Roots and Wings

There are only two bequests we need to give our children.
One is roots. The other is wings.
Author unknown

"**M**ama, I have some news," I said apprehensively. "We're moving again. Pretty far away this time."

I dreaded her response. I knew my mother's words would affect me, and either encourage or discourage my feelings about the move.

"Where are you going?"

"To the other side of the world—Phoenix, Arizona! Bill has a wonderful opportunity with the corporate office. His company is flying us out there in a couple of weeks to look for a house."

I will never forget the first words Mama spoke. "O Susan," she said with excitement in her voice, "that's wonderful! I've always wanted to go to Phoenix. Now I'll have a reason to see that part of the country!"

Her positive response not only gave me the encouragement I wanted and needed, but there were no strings of guilt attached to my leaving. There was a healthy freeing up in my heart that cleared the road ahead. As deeply rooted as I am in my family and the south, Mama and Daddy have always given me the wings to soar and move forward with my life. They have always given me "roots and wings."

It wasn't that way for Mama. My grandmother wasn't supportive when she left her home in South Carolina and moved to Florida with Daddy. So, from the time I first got married, she told me that she would always give me "roots and wings" when I moved. The roots of home and family would always be there for me, but they wanted me to have the wings to fly away and have my own life and family.

I have two paintings hanging on the wall in my office. One is of the ocean and the beach along the Florida coast, the other of a seagull with outstretched wings. They are reminders of my roots and wings. As Dr. John Trent says in *LifeMapping*, such momentos are "a tangible reminder of the process you've been through. It's a memorial marker that can give you a picture of all you can become."[1] I am deeply grateful to Mama and Daddy for the impact their gift of stability and freedom has had on my life. As Ginger and Bill, Jr. each get married within the next few months, we will be giving to them the gift my parents gave me—roots and wings.

Sometimes it's hard to imagine how a simple statement from a parent to a child rings in his or her mind for years to come. We may not know it at that moment, but the things we say and do influence our children forever—even in their moves.

Moving Really Is a Big Deal

According to the U.S. Bureau of the Census, each year over nine million children ages 1 to 14, and over two million teenagers aged 15 to 19 pack up their belongings and unpack them again in a different home.[2]

Whether they move down the street or 3,000 miles away, children need roots to anchor and support them emotionally. They need to know they have an unwavering foundation in the midst of change. Moving is difficult for children because it involves the loss of friends, school, and the familiar things that are a part of their everyday life. An article in *Parents* magazine states that "toddlers will mourn the loss of their room and of the house they've always lived in. Schoolage children will mourn the loss of their friends and the loss of their school. Teenagers, along with mourning all of the above, are likely to feel anger at their parents for a major life change that is beyond their control."[3]

Many times the move is harder for teens than for younger children. For them, a move comes at a time when they are trying to establish their independence, and they are at an age when friends are so important.

Gina, a moving friend with three boys who are 9, 12, and 14, offers this sugggestion, "During the first few months, allow for extra one-on-one talk time with each child. Be vulnerable and tell them about the ups and downs of your day and how you are feeling about the move. They learn to cope with changes as they see how you handle similar situations."

Here are some additional guidelines to help your children make the transition more smoothly:

- Don't play down the importance of the changes your children are going through.
- Telling them everything will work out isn't necessarily the best approach.
- Encourage them to express their fears and concerns. If they are too young to verbalize their feelings, help them.
- Ask your teenagers to tell you what they are feeling.
- Listen and let them do the talking.
- Don't feel that you have to justify or defend the move, shoulder the blame, or solve their problems.
- Be available to talk, listen, and provide support.
- Introduce change in stages.
- If your child lashes out in anger, acknowledge his or her feelings.
- Explain that they are reacting normally to loss.
- Don't deny your children's feelings; that intensifies their sense of isolation.
- Remember, it's normal for them to experience some temporary regression in behavior. They may even have a slight drop in grades.

In addition to the emotional adjustment of moving, children have to deal with two other types of adjustments—social and academic.

Transferring from one school to another can seem overwhelming to children. "It not only tests their academic skills, but forces them to reevaluate who they are and where they fit in. The changes in their lives and relationships can lead to feelings of isolation and failure, or to feelings of greater competency and higher self-esteem. Most will tell you that the social changes are more frightening, more difficult, and more important."⁴

A principal of a high school tells this story about a boy from Japan who was transferring to the United States for his senior year. Academically, the student was at the top of his class, but he worried about being accepted at the new school. He made a genuine effort to get involved. He wanted to be valedictorian, but was afraid that even though he was academically qualified, he might not be chosen. At that high school of 2,000, the valedictorian was selected by a commitee of other top students. He didn't think he'd have a chance. But by the end of the year, when the students with the highest averages met to decide who would represent their class as the speaker at graduation, they chose him. When he delivered his commencement speech it was about friendship. Before long, everyone in the audience was wiping their eyes.

According to a study in the journal *American Association for Counseling and Development*, it takes a new student an average of 23 days to make friends.⁵ Don't panic. That doesn't mean no one will talk to a new student or interact with him or her. It just means the friend-making process takes time.

Here are some suggestions for helping your children make a smooth transition both academically and socially. Encourage your children to:

- Be patient. It's not fun to feel like an outsider, but eventually you will find your niche. Don't be so eager to make friends that you join up with people who don't have the same values.
- Be friendly. Don't wait for others to approach you. Compliment someone on what he or she is wearing.
- Ask a classmate a question about homework or a test.
- Ask if you can sit with someone during lunch.
- Join in. Sign up for sports, drama, music, or whatever interests you.
- Don't belittle activities at your new school, even if they aren't cool by your old school's standards.
- Don't brag. If your old school or your old town was better than your new one, don't constantly compare. No one wants to hear that what they are and have is second-best.
- Observe how other kids dress. It might help you feel more socially acceptable if you know what's in.
- Expect some differences between this school and the one where you last attended. If your class is covering a subject you haven't studied or if the class is ahead of where you were at your old school, don't bluff it. Ask for help.

I remember sitting in our hotel room during the first two weeks of a hot Phoenix summer, going through the yellow pages. I was looking for any soccer leagues that Bill, Jr. and Ginger could join. They both loved soccer, and I knew the quicker I could get them involved, the better. We didn't know our way around the city, but with a map, we managed to find the soccer fields.

As I look back, getting them involved in a group activities even before school started was a springboard to their adjustment. We had visited the schools ahead of time to acclimate the children; but even so, the morning I drove up to the entrance and dropped them off at the door, I saw the apprehension in their eyes. I gave them a big smile and an even bigger hug, and said, "I know you'll have a great first day! Remember I love you. Now go for it!" I left them in God's hands then, just as I do today. I asked Him to protect, guide, and equip them in their new journey.

Accentuate the Positive

Remind your children that moving usually turns out to be a positive experience. They will see new places, meet new people, and make new friends. They will be learning new things about themselves and discovering strengths they never knew they had. The adventure of change will bring about opportunities, challenges, and great experiences. And most important, the shared experiences of moving can bring your family closer together because they will need to rely on each other. Just remember— minimize the negative and accentuate the positive! Your attitude and outlook are contagious!

♥ Heart Talk ♥

May we have another hearttalk right about now? Let's get back to talking about roots and wings for a moment. Yes, it's meaningful to give you all the facts about children moving and suggestions on helping them adjust, but the heart of the matter extends back to something far more significant.

You see, what Mama and Daddy gave me went deeper than knowing I had a family and a home that would always be there for me. They gave me a Christian foundation in which my roots could grow deep in the love of Jesus Christ. To be anchored in Christ is the basic security our children need for any transition in life. When they grow up and fly away, children will take with them the knowledge of Christ, which has been deeply rooted within.

Sometimes they may get lost and fly in the wrong direction, but eventually they will come back home to the roots of a loving God.

"Train up a child in the way he should go; even when he is old he will not depart from it" (Prov. 22:6).

"And you shall love the Lord your God with all your heart and with all your soul and with all your might. And these words, which I am commanding you today, shall be on your heart; and you shall teach them diligently to your sons and shall talk of them when you sit in your house and when you walk by the way and when you lie down and when you rise up" (Deut. 6:5-7).

"So I have also dedicated him to the Lord; as long as he lives he is dedicated to the Lord" (1 Sam. 1:28).

Pass It On

As you are providing the roots in Christ for your children, the next seven steps are vital in their growth.

1. *Principles of faith.* Base your values on the word of God (Col. 2: 6-7).

2. *Pattern of life.* Strive to live a life worthy of imitation that models God's design (Eph. 5:1-2).

3. *Persistence that is immovable.* Don't give up. Don't let anything move you from what you believe. Be strong in your faith (Eph. 6:10, 14).

4. *Participation.* Feel what your children feel. Laugh when they laugh. Cry when they cry. Learn with them (Rom. 12:15).

5. *Praise.* Encourage them. Believe in them. Sing *to* them when they are small. Sing *with* them when they are grown (Phil. 4:4-5).

6. *Prayer.* Let them see you pray, hear you pray, and watch you give God the credit for the results (Phil. 4:6).

7. *Planning.* It's never too late. Plan on giving them roots and wings! (Isa. 40:31, Deut. 32:11)

My dear friend and sister in Christ, Donna Otto, says in her wonderful book *The Stay at Home Mom,* "What your child becomes in the future will reflect how you shape them, nurture them, and discipline them today."[6] Begin today laying the foundation for tomorrow!

A Parable for Mothers

The young mother set her foot on the path of life. "Is the way long?" she asked. And her guide said, "Yes, the way is hard. And you will be old before you reach the end of it. But the end will be better than the beginning."

But the young mother was happy, and she would not believe that anything could be better than these years. So she played with her children, and gathered flowers for them along the way, and bathed with them in the clear streams, and the sun shone on them, and life was good, and the young mother cried, "Nothing will ever be lovelier than this."

Then night came, and the storm, and the path was dark, and the children shook with fear and cold, and the mother drew them close and covered them with her mantle, and the children said, "O Mother, we are not afraid, for you are near, and no harm can come," and the mother said, "This is better than the brightness of day, for I have taught my children courage."

The morning came and there was a hill ahead, and the children climbed and grew weary, and the mother was weary, but at all times she said to the children, "A little patience, and we are there." So the children climbed, and when they reached the top they said, "We could not have done it without you, Mother."

The mother, when she lay down that night, looked up at the stars and said, "This is a better day than the last, for my children have learned fortitude in the face of hardness. Yesterday I gave them courage. Today I have given them strength."

The next day came strange clouds which darkened the earth—clouds of war and hate and evil—and the children groped and stumbled, and the mother said, "Look up. Lift your eyes to the Light." And the children looked and saw above the darkness. And in the night the mother said, "This is the best day of all, for I have shown my children God."

The mother grew old, but her children were tall and strong and walked with courage. And the mother said, "I have reached the end of my journey. Now I know that the end is better than the beginning. For my children can walk alone, and their children after them."

The children said, "You will always walk with us, Mother, even when you have gone through the golden gates."

They stood and watched her as she went on alone, and the gates at the end of the shining road closed after her. And they said, "We cannot see her, but she is with us still. A mother like ours is more than a memory. She is a Living Presence."[7]

"Her children arise and call her blessed" (Prov. 31:28, NIV).

I'll get up out of my hammock to welcome you to the next chapter! That's how excited I am to share with you all about making friends after a move!

Survival Kit

Twenty ways to help your children adjust after a move:

1. Christen your new home by tying a big bow—for each child on the front door. When a child cuts his or her bow, take a picture to put in your moving day scrapbook.
2. Type your new address/phone number in columns with a two-inch margin and fold on lines above and below each address so you and the children can tear one off for friends.
3. Have a family party with cookies, punch, and talk. Remember, talk can be more refreshing than cookies and punch.
4. Don't skip breakfast. It gives them energy to start the day.
5. Encourage your kids to plant seeds or flowers in the yard. Explain how we all have to root and grow in new soil.
6. Encourage them to invite friends home after school. You provide the pizza.
7. Establish routine as quickly as possible.
8. Don't do away with old toys and familiar possessions. They may give your child a feeling of continuity.
9. Let your child take part in decorating his or her room.
10. Begin new traditions in this new house.
11. Listen, listen, listen. Don't preach or teach; instead give your kids lots of hugs.
12. Let them mourn their losses in the move.
13. Get them involved in a good youth program at church.
14. Write "I love U" or "Have a great day!" on the napkin in their lunchboxes or on a piece of paper tucked in their notebooks.
15. Allow each child a five-minute, long-distance call to a friend back in the old town.
16. Give them lots of reassurance.

17. Pray for them every day.
18. Tuck them in at bedtime.
19. Give them roots in Christ, family, and home.
20. Give them wings of freedom to move forward in their journey of life.

Chapter 15

Borrow an Egg

Won't you be my neighbor? Won't you please, won't you please,
please won't you be my neighbor?
Theme song from "Mister Roger's Neighborhood"

I have comforted many a newcomer in my hammock after a move has left them friendless. It's in my hammock that I have been consoled in my own emptiness after moving. It's also been a place where new friendships have been formed and old ones enriched. I can think of no better place for us to talk about friendship than in my hammock.

"We used to talk on the phone every day," Chris shared with me as we began to swing gently. "Beth was closer to me than a sister. She was so much a part of my life. We understood each other's feelings and thoughts; we knew what the other was going to say even before she said it. There wasn't anything we wouldn't do for one another." Chris stopped the hammock from swinging with her feet, looked at me and said, "No one can ever take her place. I miss her terribly!"

The separation from her dearest friend, Beth, was devastating to Chris. I knew this wasn't the time for platitudes or shallow words, telling her she would find another close friend in time. For the moment, just the gentle sway of the hammock and my presence was enough. Chris spent the afternoon with me. We talked a lot about friendship—what a gift a close friend is to us, and how many people go through life without ever experiencing a deep, meaningful friendship. As Chris got up from the hammock, she remarked, "I look back and cherish the memories Beth and I made together. I think I'll go and write her a letter, telling her what a difference she has made in my life."

Chris and Beth's friendship remained close, and they adjusted to the distance between them. No one ever took Beth's place, but after a while one person found a special place in Chris's life.

When we move, so many of the things we leave behind can be replaced rather quickly, and life then resumes its pace with a fairly normal rhythm. Friendships are the exception. The void created by the absence of a dear friend leaves a gaping wound in our hearts, and the longing for shared intimacy keeps us out of step with the world around us.

What a Difference a Friend Makes

What is it that makes a friend a friend? Why is it that one person entwines her life and heart with ours, making "parting such sweet sorrow"?

Dee Brestin says it beautifully in her book, *The Friendships of Women*. "When I talk to my closest female friends, I feel my soul being sunned and watered when they ask questions, drawing out the deep waters of my soul, and when they empathize, rejoicing when I rejoice, weeping when I weep." [1]

Let me tell you about some friends who have knitted their lives with mine. Remember my friend Nancy from Atlanta? When we moved, I could find no one to take her place in my heart. But God did the most incredible thing—He gave me another Nancy in Phoenix! She is a friend and sister in Christ who is most precious and dear to my heart. How blessed I am to have two Nancys—one in the South and one in the West! These two have taught me about unconditional love between friends. The immeasurable love they pour over my family and me has no limit.

Then God did the most incredible thing—He just kept multiplying wonderful godly women in my life, far beyond all I could ever imagine. In addition to Nancy, God gave me women like Bev, Carol, Donna, Dottie,

Jackie, Joan, Juli, Karen, Kay, Mary K., Mary M., Mona, Sandy, Sheryl, Sudie, and Terry. These are women who sometimes walked ahead of me and led the way, sometimes walked behind me and followed, but always walked with me, holding my hand. Together, we have shared in celebration and sorrow, birth and death, divorce, illness, financial crisis, tears, and laughter. They have accepted me just as I am, encouraged me, held me accountable for my actions, affirmed my good qualities, and helped me change my bad ones. They have been sensitive to my needs, served me unabashedly, and prayed for me faithfully. But first and foremost, the foundation of our friendship is built on our common bond in Christ. We do not measure our love and devotion to one another by the world's standard of who we are, how much we have, and what we wear. Our standard is based on a Christ-centered love. We are all equal in His eyes. Our love and devotion to each other is the same love and devotion that Christ has for us. Because we have received His love, we can then give that love to others.

Jesus—Our Role Model

The best way to learn about Christian friendship is to go back to the source—the one who can impart love, the one who can model love—Jesus Christ.

No one in the scriptures said more about relationships through His actions and His words than Jesus. (Read Matthew, Mark, Luke, and John to learn all about the life of Jesus.) What a powerful role model for us! He best demonstrates an observable love for others. Jesus came to live among us so that He could relate to us and we could relate to Him. He has walked in our shoes. He has felt our pain and joy, our love and rejection, and has experienced our disappointment and despair.

If we observe the kind of relationship Jesus had with His disciples, then the basics for a Christian friendship become clear. He shared His life with them. He spent time with them. He prayed with them. He was committed to them. He built trust with them. He accepted them. He encouraged them. He was sensitive to them. He forgave them. He didn't just teach the disciples about His love; He expressed it to them in a way they could feel it and see it. His love was tangible. In other words, He didn't just talk the talk; He walked the walk!

"A new commandment I give to you, that you love one another, even as I have loved you, that you also love one another. By this all men will know that you are My disciples, if you have love for one another" (Jn. 13: 34-35). In Kathy Narramore's book on friendship, *Kindred Spirits*, she says,

> "It is as if Jesus were saying to each of us, 'You will experience my love as you love each other. You can know about my love from my Word but you are to experience it through your friendships. This will be possible not only because I will be with you, but because I will be in you, through my Spirit empowering you.' It seems God planned for us to do our spiritual and emotional maturing in relationships with others. Growth takes place in the context of relationships. Christian friendships are designed to promote our growth toward maturity by helping us see God and ourselves. They can also help meet our deep emotional needs as we accept, care for, encourage, forgive, and are committed to one another. As we do this for one another, we reflect the Lord to one another." [2]

Look for This Kind of Friend

Jesus is the best friend you can have. You can always lean on Him, and He'll never back away from you. No matter where you move, He's the friend waiting on you with open arms. You see, He wants to be on the inside, and wants you to have Christian friends on the outside—friends who can put their arms around you and remind you that you are loved. Friends who can say encouraging words to you. Friends who can reflect His love for you in a visible way. Look for a friend who is an extension of Jesus Christ, not a substitute for Him. Look for someone who will love you unconditionally and accept you as you are, as she points you toward Jesus. Look for a friend who will walk with you through thick and thin, as she reminds you that Jesus cares and understands. Feel His presence through your friends.

This is the kind of friend you need to look for:

- Someone you can laugh with.
- Someone you can pray with.
- Someone you can share your heart with.
- Someone you can trust.
- Someone who will respond at a time of need.
- Someone you can share experiences with.

I love the way Jerry and Mary White describe a friend in their book, *Friends & Friendship*. "A friend is a trusted confidant to whom I am mutually drawn as a companion and an ally, whose love for me is not dependent on my performance, and whose influence draws me closer to God."[3]

A Story of Four Friends

This is a story of four newcomers who found the love of Jesus Christ through their friendship. Margie and Joan were sitting together at their sons' Little League game when Joan asked Margie how her day was going. Margie burst into tears as they talked, and later on in the conversation, Joan suggested that Margie join her at a newcomer's class at her church. When Margie walked into the room, she felt welcomed and accepted. It was through that class that she later discovered a personal relationship with the Lord.

The friendship between Margie and Joan became very special and unique. Joan was never hesitant to speak about the Lord, to suggest praying about things, to give of her time unselfishly, and to always be available. Joan and Margie were always there for each other as faithful friends and prayer partners. They held one another accountable and knew that in a crisis they could depend on each other, day or night. They accepted one another completely and knew they could be themselves, no matter what happened.

When Joan moved it was very hard on both of them. Margie said that God didn't remove a friend from her life; He simply put them in a different phase of their friendship. Although they are geographically far apart, they continue to stay in close touch by writing and talking on the phone.

They still feel part of each other's life. They still feel they are there for each other, even across the miles. Margie said that God has been faithful to keep their friendship intact and has even made it grow stronger. Then she said, "We don't know where our lives will lead us, but we do know that God put us together for a reason, and that He will be faithful to us. It's the spiritual bonding that has truly kept our friendship so special and unique."

Two other newcomers, Debby and Jan, have a similar story. They met through the newcomer's group at church. Debby said, "I'm so thankful for Jan. She is my best friend and is as close as a sister to me. When we met, I was new to motherhood, to marriage, to church, and to God's love. I'll never forget when Jan walked up to me and asked to come over to see some crafts I was making at the time. From that moment on, God has blessed me with the most rewarding sisterhood. I thank God every day for her. Through our friendship I have grown in my walk with Christ."

The wonderful story of their friendship continued as Debby moved away for several years and then moved back to Phoenix! They visited each other across the miles and stayed in touch, not knowing they would be reunited in an even closer relationship.

What encouraging stories of four newcomers who found a lasting friendship established in Christ that neither time nor distance will diminish!

Making New Friends

Were you a little bit curious about my chapter title, "Borrow an Egg"? Well, you see, it all boils down to how to make new friends! Several years ago, when some of my friends moved, I took them a special little going-away present. I put these items in a cute little pink gift bag with pink tissue paper tucked inside: a small bird's nest with tiny eggs (from a craft store); an egg (I buy the plastic or wooden ones on sale after Easter); a bookmark that says, "Bloom where you're planted!"; a small mirror; and a six-inch piece of white rope with a pink ribbon tied around it.

As I gave it to them I would say, "The first thing you must do when you move is to make your nest a home! Weave it with love and happiness. Second, borrow an egg. This is the easiest way to meet your neighbor and start a friendship. Third, put this bookmark in your Bible as a reminder to find a church. After that, you must look in this mirror as a reminder that it all begins with you. And finally, hold on tight to this rope. It is woven with God's love, His Word, and His promises."

Many of my friends have written that they still have these little reminders and have followed these simple steps to help them adjust. Can you pretend that I just gave that going away gift to you? Let it be a reminder that I care about you in your move, just as I do about my other moving friends.

♥ Heart Talk ♥

In addition to my love for flowers, birds and hammocks, I love the beach. I've collected seashells from the beach for many years. Come with me, and we will stroll the beach and look for seashells as we have our heart talk.

Seashells are a lot like friends. No two are exactly alike; they're all one of a kind! I love adding new shells, as well as new friends, to those I already have. I find shells scattered along the beach. I find friends along the shores of life. Sometimes it takes a lot of time and effort to find special shells and special friends. I always take the shells and the friends with me, everywhere

I go. Each has lasting value to me, and I treasure the memories of where and how I found them. May your life be enriched and blessed by the friends you find along the life's shoreline as you move.

Survival Kit

Twenty-one ways to make new friends:

1. Be approachable.
2. Take the opportunities God gives you. When someone invites you to do something this week, invite them to do something next week.
3. Talk to other shoppers about the price of lettuce (or whatever) in the grocery store.
4. When you are invited to do things, say "yes" even though you feel shy, don't know how to get to the invite's house, or don't know what to wear.
5. Offer to carpool.
6. Send a card or a note to someone who needs to be encouraged.
7. Be available.
8. Invite someone to lunch.
9. Join a women's Bible study.
10. Pray for God to send just the right person to be your friend.
11. Find a need in your church or community and fill it.
12. Walk your children to the bus stop and talk to other mothers.
13. Be yourself.
14. Be an initiator.
15. Be a good listener.
16. Put on a happy face and smile.
17. Find something you have in common with people you meet.
18. Ask questions.
19. Find a church.
20. Remember, to have a friend, you must be a friend!
21. Sometimes, to make friends, all you need to do is show up.

PART III

Move Ahead

As we walked together through the process of starting over in Part Two, you began to have a new hope for yourself, a new attitude about your home, and a new relationship with your family. It is my prayer that you have made the choice to allow God to mold you through this process. If you've done that during this transition, you truly have made a new beginning. Now you are ready to begin the last process and move ahead.

As I made the choice to go forward, I began to take the focus off myself and concentrate more on God and on others in my life. It was time to come full circle by finding contentment in the midst of my circumstances, by developing a more balanced life, and by starting to reach out to others. I came to know more intimately the One who moves with me.

Because I had allowed God to MEND and MOLD me, He could then MATURE me in my walk with Him. I invite you to join me and move onward in this last process as we continue our journey. This is the bow that ties the book together.

> To let go—allows God to mend you!
> To start over—allows God to mold you!
> To move ahead—allows God to mature you!

Chapter 16

Coming Full Circle

The Lord's lovingkindnesses indeed never cease,
for His compassions never fail. They are new every morning;
great is Thy faithfulness.
Lamentations 3:22-23

Before you go any further, I want you to stop and give yourself a big
HUG from me! You probably don't realize how close you are to
being able to carry on with your life because of your decision to let go and
start over. It must be like a breath of fresh air to realize that by processing
those two stages, you are going to be all right!

Just between the two of us—I believe in you! I am confident in who you
are. I strongly feel you are going to make it. You have already come this far.
I am certain you are a different person from the inside out. You have taken
the time to examine your life, to address your heart, and to get a new
perspective on your move.

Look in the Right Direction

There are three things on my heart that are essential for coming full circle. Each of these things come from within and will significantly affect your life. They are the ability to:

1. Live above your circumstances. Robin had moved seven times in seven years of marriage. One of those moves was particularly difficult as she faced many hardships. She had dealt with cancer, a new baby, marital conflicts, and now the move was one more stress added to her life.

Robin chose to let go, start over, and move ahead. She has come full circle in her process of moving and has begun to focus on God's faithfulness and steadfastness, not on the circumstances that surround her life.

2. Live in contentment. Sudie's 10th move was to California. This move, however, was different from the others. Although the adjustment was difficult, Sudie felt peace and tranquility, which she knew didn't come from her circumstances. Both Sudie and her husband, Raleigh, came full circle through the moving process. Because he became more aware of what a woman goes through emotionally during a moving transition, Raleigh was more understanding and sensitive to Sudie's needs than ever before. Their marriage relationship grew stronger and they bonded even more during this difficult time. Raleigh realized that a move isn't just something you do; it's something you feel.

3. Live with joy. Beverly has moved to nine different states. Even now, she knows a company transfer is inevitable. She also knows how to roll with the punches! I have never seen anyone move with such ease. She takes it all in stride and does what has to be done to settle in quickly. She doesn't resent the moves or hold any bitterness in her heart about moving so much. She lives with a joy that isn't dependent on her circumstances. She understands how important the process of letting go, starting over, and moving ahead is in her transition.

What do these three women have in common? How do they live above circumstances? Live in contentment? Live with joy? They have made a choice to keep God as the focus in their life, not the circumstances around them. Their focus is vertical, not horizontal. They have learned to respond first to God, instead of to people and situations.

In *The Beauty of Beholding God*, Darien Cooper says, "Marriage, career, children, social status, possessions, and even friends do not satisfy the inner

void in our lives. They are meant to be enjoyed, but none are life-giving." [1]
Only a relationship with Jesus Christ can fill the void in your life. Jesus says,
"I am the way, and the truth, and the life" (Jn. 14:6).

On a Clear Day, I Can See Forever

It's only when you live above your circumstances, by changing the focus
of your life, that serenity and joy can come to you. You see, my friend, when
you concentrate on who God is by knowing Him personally, then you will
understand His peace and security. He doesn't always change your situation;
what He does is give you new strength and hope so you can face those
circumstances and keep on going. "Look not at the things which are seen,
but at the things which are not seen; for the things which are seen are
temporal, but the things which are not seen are eternal" (2 Cor. 4:18).

Maybe you didn't want to move and leave your friends. Maybe you are
terribly lonely. Maybe your marriage is suffering from the transition. Maybe
your children are rebelling over moving. Regardless of your circumstances,
you can rest, secure in the faithfulness of God. He does not change. "Jesus
Christ is the same yesterday and today, yes and forever" (Heb. 13:8); "Cast
all your anxiety on Him, because He cares for you" (1 Pet. 5:7, NIV).

My friend Mary often says when any of us are in crisis, "Do you walk by
faith or by sight?" It sure brings us back to center very quickly. Yes, I'll walk
by faith any day! I know God sees the big picture of my life. I don't need to
know everything from beginning to end, because God already does.
Through faith in Him, I can encounter life's problems with confidence,
knowing that He will see me through. My God is bigger than whatever
circumstances may surround me! "Trust in the Lord God always, for in the
Lord Jehovah is your everlasting strength" (Isa. 26:4, LB).

♥   Heart Talk   ♥

Let's take a break and heart talk. If you were to ask me what you should
do about your situation, I would tell you to look beyond your circumstances.
Look past them, just as if you were standing on the shore, peering across the
water to the solid soil on the other side. The circumstances in your life are
the water, and God is your safe and solid ground. He uses everything possible to bring you across that water to Him.

Sometimes you may get distracted and go off course. Just remember to
keep your eyes fastened on Him. Don't let the water take you under. Keep

paddling. Once you reach the other side and look back, you'll have a greater understanding of your journey. "And you will seek Me and find Me, when you search for Me with all your heart" (Jer. 29:13).

Desert Experiences

How many times have you said, "If only . . . it sure would make this move a lot easier"? One of my moving friends, Dianna, put it best when she said, "'If only' is a delusion. It's being discontent with what God has provided."

How many of you have had a dry period of discontentment—a "desert experience" after you settled in? That's a pretty normal part of the moving process for most of us!

After the dust settles, reality hits. That's when it's easy to look around and compare, or think about all the "if onlys," or all the "have nots." The dust does settle and the desert experiences do come. Expect them and don't be so hard on yourself! You're not always going to be happy. You're not always going to be up. You're not always going to have it all together. And you're certainly not always going to feel spiritual! You are a woman in process, not a woman who is a perfect, finished product.

Don't Worry—Be Happy

One of the best definitions of contentment is in Philippians 4:11-12, "Not that I speak from want; for I have learned to be content in whatever circumstances I am. I know how to get along with humble means, and I also know how to live in prosperity; in any and every circumstance I have learned the secret of being filled and going hungry, both of having abundance and suffering need." Read it again. Do you know the secret to Paul's contentment? It's being satisfied with what God has or has not given you. I know that all moves are not up the ladder. Some are down the ladder, with job losses and company cut backs happening all across the nation. You might have had to adjust to a lesser income, a smaller home, and fewer possessions. Can you say, "It is well with my soul," in spite of your circumstances?

Bill and I have experienced downsizing in recent years. We've discovered, just like Paul, that "God shall supply all your needs according to His riches in glory in Christ Jesus" (Phil. 4:19). Bill has said many times, "God may not supply all our wants, but He sure has supplied all our needs over the last few years!"

How do you learn contentment? First of all, detach your happiness from your circumstances. Happiness comes from inside your heart. Happiness from within produces contentment, regardless of your circumstances. From that contentment comes peace. I know. I have experienced that peace over the years.

Next, abide. Yes, simply abide. Abide in God's word. Read John 14 and 15. Abide in prayer. Abide in His promises. Just abide in Him. It works wonders. Then, focus on real things that have lasting value —family, relationships, health, friends, and the Lord.

Finally, realize everything you have is a gift from God through His grace in your life. Accept it, whether it be much or little. It is sufficient.

I Have That Joy, Joy, Joy, Joy Down in My Heart!

In Tim Hansel's incredible book *You Gotta Keep Dancin'*, he says that "Joy . . . occurs in spite of difficult situations. It is not a feeling; it is a choice. It is not based upon circumstances; it is based upon attitude." [2] He quotes Paul Sailhamer who said, "Joy is that deep settled confidence that God is in control of every area of my life." [3]

Joy surpasses happiness and keeps on going deep within—so deep that it permeates our whole demeanor. Joy can be seen in our eyes, our smile, even the way we walk. It's an outward expression of an inner relationship with God. "These things I have spoken to you, that My joy may be in you, and *that* your joy may be made full" (Jn. 15:11).

Tribute to a Smile

When I think of someone who chooses joy in her life, I remember a former newcomer, Vicki. One of the special qualities about Vicki was her beautiful smile. When she moved here, she was married and had a young daughter. Then, her husband left her. Every time I saw Vicki at church with her daughter, she was smiling. She had chosen to be joyful in spite of her circumstances. It was obvious that her joy was an expression of God's presence in her life. Then, Vicki was diagnosed with cancer. Even then, every time I saw her, she had that radiant smile woven with joy and peace on her face. I talked to Vicki the other day. She's bedridden at home now. The cancer has slowly taken over her body, but it hasn't taken her smile, nor her joy, nor her unshakable faith in God. Vicki has taught me about real joy.

By reading this chapter, you will better understand how to:

Live above your circumstances
Live in contentment
Live with joy
. . . as you make the transition in your move.

Congratulations! You are in the process of coming full circle, and now ready to move ahead! In the next chapter we're going to be equipped to head in a new direction.

Chapter 17

Back in the Saddle Again!

In everything you do, put God first, and He will direct you
and crown your efforts with success.
Proverbs 3:6, TLB

As I reached for a head of lettuce in my grocery store's produce section, I noticed that lettuce is also conveniently sold cut up in bags. It looked like a smart, practical way to buy lettuce. The bag even had a nice lock-top, so you could use a little and keep the rest fresh.

But, when I shop for lettuce, I *always* pick up every head, examining each to get the best and heaviest one. So, instead of the pre-packaged salad, I once again bought a head of lettuce, because I'm a creature of habit. I'm often reluctant to change my routine. Some habits are worth keeping but some need a good cleaning out.

Are you, too, a creature of habit? Do you find it hard to change old ways? Many aspects of your life may need to be examined and weighed to see if change is necessary. They may be important matters of the heart or just minor things in the course of a day that need rethinking or revising since you've moved.

Now is the time to "turn over a new leaf." What a great opportunity to make some changes that will give you new direction, and make your life easier and more enjoyable.

Take One Giant Step

I can never pass up a scrumptious muffin. It's really hard for me to stick to a diet, because I can't find one that says, "You are allowed one scrumptious muffin a day." (The difference between a scrumptious muffin and a regular muffin is that the scrumptious one is twice as big as the other and has crispy edges—it's irresistible!) So, I've just decided to collect diets instead of going on them. I now have a file full of diets!

All this muffin talk is just to say I'm not very self-disciplined when it comes to dieting. Or when it comes to writing, either. It's hard for me to get to my office (which is in my home) at a set time each day to begin writing. I can find 10 things to do while walking from the bedroom to the office. And when I sit down, I find five more reasons to get up! Maybe talking about self-discipline will help me as well as you!

The giant step of self-discipline will be the springboard for setting new goals, new priorities, and doing some reorganizing. In Earl Wilson's book *Self-Discipline*, he states, "Self-discipline is nothing more than a series of small choices which protect the minutes of your life, allowing you to become a more productive person."[1]

I have a moving friend who works at night as a nurse and is the mother of four children. After she gets home from work, she sends them off to school. Then before she goes to work at night, she gets them ready for bed. It requires a lot of self-discipline to manage a schedule like that, but she is committed to making it work. Philippians 3:13-14 gives me some bibical insights regarding self-discipline. "I do not regard myself as having laid hold of it yet; but one thing I do: forgetting what lies behind and reaching forward to what lies ahead, I press on toward the goal for the prize of the upward call of God in Christ Jesus."

Do you see the four key phrases in these verses which are necessary for self-discipline? They are: one thing, forgetting, reaching forward, and press on.

"One thing" means I need to be single-minded and focus on what I'm trying to accomplish. Doing 10 things at once is definitely a distraction from my primary goal.

"Forgetting" indicates putting something out of my mind. I need to clear my mind of less important things so that I can be free to do what is most significant.

"Reaching forward" involves stretching or extending myself. At times I feel like I'm trying to do something that's out of reach; but the more I stretch toward the goal, the closer I come to achieving it.

"Press on" means to go forward with effort and commitment. Worthwhile goals aren't simply going to happen. They must be pursued with determination.

My daddy told me when I got married, "You can find out everything you need to know about how to live your life—everything from spending money to being a good wife to raising children—all in the Bible. That's the best manual you can have." I continue to get wonderful direction, for even the smallest things, right within its pages. I even find instruction for self-discipline and setting goals.

You know now the first step in making any change is to exercise self-discipline. I like the way Dale Hanson Bourke says it, "Discipline often makes the difference between what we want to be and what we actually are." [2]

I have often admired my friend Sheryl's self-discipline and perserverance. After moving to Phoenix, she went back to school for a degree in interior design. I encourage you to rethink and reflect on any area of your life that you feel might need a change, either personal or spiritual. This may be just the right time to turn things around.

Be a Trailblazer

Why don't we blaze a trail with some goal-setting? It'll be a lot easier knowing we are doing it together! There are markers along the trail to help us as we pursue our goals. Let's see what they are:

Marker 1. Write it down! Otherwise, you don't have a goal, only a wish. When you see a goal written down, it becomes a reality. (I'm going to write down exactly how much weight I want to lose by a specific date.)

Marker 2. Have a plan! Without a specific plan, you'll find it difficult to reach your goal. (I will walk two miles every day and start counting fat grams. Do they make scrumptious fat-free muffins?)

Marker 3. Take it one day at a time! Trying to achieve too much all at once can be overwhelming. (I'll set goals of five-pound increments. Having to lose as much as I need to could look overwhelming and I might give up.)

Marker 4. Be good to yourself! If you've reached a goal, you deserve a reward. (When I do lose five pounds, I'll celebrate!)

Marker 5. Don't give up! Keep your ultimate goal in mind. (Even if I cheat on my diet, I'll start right back on it the very same day.)

Thoreau said, "Go ahead and build your castles in the air. That's where they belong. Now put some foundations under them." [3]

Goals of the Heart

Some of the most significant goals I've made are spiritual ones. These are goals from my heart. After a move, you can make changes not only in your personal life, but also in your spiritual life.

When I made the move to Phoenix, I wanted to read and study the Bible all the more. I had come to a different place and stage in my life and I found certain verses, no matter how many times I had read them in the past, had new meaning after the move. I wanted to find a Bible study where I could grow deeper through God's word and through fellowship with other women.

I wanted to cultivate a more faithful prayer time. Take a good look at your heart. Are there any changes that need to take place? *Think not just about what you will do; think about who you will become.*

The Heart of the Matter

Let's go a little deeper into the heart. In Joseph Allison's book *Setting Goals That Count*, he talks about how God influences your goal-setting and plan-making through your internal guidance system, which the Bible refers to as the heart.[4] God guides you through your heart. The Bible reveals that your internal guidance system has two interrelated functions. The heart function refers to setting goals and forming character. The mind function deals with making daily plans to reach your goals. Look at the difference between a person's heart and mind in this verse, "I will put my laws into their minds, and I will write them upon their hearts. And I will be their God, and they shall be My people" (Heb. 8:10).

Notice that it says God will put (suggesting temporary keeping) His law into their minds, and write (suggesting permanent keeping) it upon their hearts. We often say that we've changed our mind, but seldom do we say we've changed our heart. A person's heart guides what his or her mind thinks.

Jesus taught that the heart guides our entire life (Matt. 12:34; Mark 7:21-23; Luke 6:43-45). It's the switchboard for our thoughts, feelings, and actions. If we change our heart, we change our entire life. God can transform your life by giving you a new heart with new goals.

A Changed Heart

From the moment Laurie walked into our newcomer's class, there was skepticism written all over her face. She couldn't quite figure out whether or not we were for real. Laurie had never experienced unconditional love and she didn't quite know how to accept it. She had heard of Jesus Christ, but didn't know Him personally. She asked me to come over to her house weekly, "Just to answer some questions," she said. She talked, I listened. I talked, she listened. We read scripture. We prayed. But I could tell that her heart just wasn't ready. She couldn't accept how simple and uncomplicated the love of Christ actually is.

She quit coming to class, but we kept calling her. She always had an excuse for why she couldn't come. Finally, she said there was no point in our meeting anymore, so we stopped. Ocasionally, I saw her in the grocery store, but that was all the contact we had.

One morning two years later, the phone rang and it was Laurie. "Can I come over?" she said. "I have something to tell you."

When Laurie walked in the front door, I could see it all over her face. She was a different person. She smiled and embraced me. "I just had to see you," she said. "You see, I started going to this small church nearby, and then I got involved in a Bible study, and now I know Christ!" By this time my eyes were brimming with tears. "The reason I had to see you was to ask for your forgiveness."

"My forgiveness?"

"Yes," she said. "All of you were so loving and kind to me in class, and my heart was so hardened. And then you wouldn't give up on me and you put up with all my rebellion against God. I know God has forgiven me, and I want you to forgive me too."

"O Laurie," I said, and we both started to cry. "Yes, of course I'll forgive you." The change was so obvious, it showed in her eyes, her smile and her voice. I was touched by her desire to seek my forgiveness.

She left that day, and I haven't seen her since. But I was once again reminded of God's powerful, life-changing love, and how in some small way, He allowed me to be a part of Laurie's journey to find Him. Talk about making a change—Laurie did just that!

♥   Heart Talk   ♥

"I think I can, I think I can," said The Little Engine That Could. Before you start huffing and puffing to make changes, to become more self-disciplined, or to set new goals, let me share some thoughts to keep you on track.

You are starting over with a clean calendar. You have no regular commitments and no hectic schedules. Choose carefully how you fill your calendar. Now is the time to take a good look at what you put back into your life. It's a good time to make different choices than you have in the past. Perhaps you need to check your priorities and make sure they are in the right order. You can choose to unclutter and uncomplicate your life! Perhaps you were overcommitted before you moved. What a great time to reevaluate what's most important to you!

It's time for you to "come back to center," as I say when I feel myself getting off track with my life. My "center" is God. When everything pivots around Him, I'm on track. When I try to fit Him around everything else, my life is out of balance. Doing more doesn't usually make you a better person. Ask yourself if what you are doing is right for you and for your marriage and family. Being busy isn't necessarily being productive. Maybe you just need to step back and take a deep breath before you plunge into life again. It's good for your soul to stop and smell the flowers, to watch a sunset.

Be who you are and strive to be a better you. Don't waste a single move. Grow, learn, and change from your move. Understand that you don't have to have it all together. Just try to remember where you put what you've got! (My spices aren't organized alphabetically and my pictures aren't put away in albums, but I know where they are!)

Are you moving in the right direction? You'll know in the next chapter.

Survival Kit

To make your life run more smoothly:

- Establish a family message center. Use it for shopping lists, phone messages, calendars, reminders.
- Use plastic ice cube trays to store earrings in your jewelry drawer.

- Attach jewelry pins to an old T-shirt and hang on a hanger.
- Hang necklaces on wooden pegs.
- Put cardboard between sets of placemats so you can remove one set without disturbing the others.
- Hang tablecloths on sturdy hangers.
- Store napkin rings by sets in lock-top bags.
- Store socks, belts, gloves, scarves, stockings, and underwear in pocketed shoe bags.
- Invest in an assortment of hooks, dividers, clear boxes, and other containers that make it easy to keep things separate and quick to find.
- Start a general subject file on everything from A to Z that involves your life and interests. Mine starts with antiques and ends with weddings.
- Use the space under a skirted table to store things. I put small things under there that have to be temporarily put away to make room for Christmas decorations.
- Add an extra shelf in any unused space at the top of the closet.
- Add another garment pole above the existing one for hanging shorter items like blouses or skirts.

Chapter 18

A Move in
the Right Direction

*I find the great thing in this world is not so much where we stand
as in what direction we are moving.*
Oliver Wendell Holmes

When I was a little girl, Mama and I went on a trip to South Carolina. We stopped at a little country gas station in the middle of nowhere, and Mama rolled down the window to ask an old gentleman sitting in a chair in front of the station, "Excuse me, sir. Could you tell me how much further it is?"

He replied, "Well, ma'am, it all depends on where you're comin' from and where you're goin' to." She realized how funny her question was, and we all laughed together. Mama then gave him the rest of the information, and he told her how far we had to go.

His words often come back to my mind. I ask myself every now and then, *Where am I comin' from and where am I goin' to?* to make sure I'm moving in the right direction. Since our journey will soon be coming to an end, let me ask you, "Do you know where you're goin' to, and are you movin' in the right direction?"

Oswald Chambers puts it all in perspective. "It is no use to pray for the old days; stand square where you are and make the present better than any past has been. Base all on your relationship to God and go forward, and presently you will find that what is emerging is infinitely better than the past ever was." [1] Write that down and put it on your refrigerator! One of my prayers for you is that your move is a rewarding change, "infinitely better than the past ever was!"

Follow the Leader

We all come from different places and different backgrounds, and that certainly affects where we're going in life. But I know one thing for sure; you're moving in the right direction if you're following the leader—Jesus Christ. To know Him is to love Him, and to follow Him is life-changing.

Remember playing Follow the Leader as a child? To play this game you did exactly what the leader did. Similarly, as Christians we are to "be imitators of God, as beloved children; and walk in love, just as Christ also loved you" (Eph. 5:1-2). Our leader, Jesus, beckons for us to follow Him. "Jesus said . . . Come, follow Me'" (Matt. 19:21). The more you read, study, observe, understand the life of Christ, and then imitate Him, the more your life will be an overflow of Him.

By imitating Christ and living a life centered on Him, your focus will shift from thinking of yourself and your circumstances to thinking of others and how you can best serve them. By refocusing, you are taking another step in the process of moving ahead—another step in the right direction.

Martha! Get Out of That Kitchen!

I can't tell you how many times I've heard over the years, "Susan, get out of that kitchen and come here! You've got to hear this." Or, "Come here, you've got to see this!" We have all been in that situation at one time or another. Because we've all missed out on what was going on by being so busy in the kitchen, we can relate to the story of the two sisters, Mary and Martha.

Martha had invited Jesus to dinner. I'm sure the home she shared with Mary and their brother Lazarus was spotless and tidy because Martha wanted everything just right for Him. While Martha was busy in the kitchen with all the details and preparations, Mary was in the other room listening to Jesus. Well, needless to say, that ticked Martha off! How could her sister be sitting in there, relaxing and listening to Jesus, when there was so much to do! I can imagine that she marched out of the kitchen in a rather huffy manner, ready to let everyone know she was knocking herself out doing everything, while they were all enjoying themselves! Then she said, "Lord, do You not care that my sister has left me to do all the serving alone? Then tell her to help me" (Luke 10:40). He didn't say, "Martha, just cool it!" No, instead Jesus replied calmly, "Martha, Martha, you are worried and bothered about so many things, but only a few things are necessary" (Luke 10:41-42).

Notice that Jesus didn't get upset with Martha for what she was doing. There's no doubt that she had a servant's heart. It was her attitude as she served that was the problem. Martha was task-oriented; Mary was Master-oriented. Martha was interested in what she was doing; Mary was interested in what she was becoming. As you begin to broaden your horizons, make new friends, and become involved in the lives of others, keep in mind the Mary and Martha story.

Jean Fleming says in her book *Between Walden and the Whirlwind*, "The Christian life should have a rhythm—doing and resting, speaking and listening, giving and receiving." She goes on to say, "Not only must God minister through us, He must minister to us."[2] What an opportunity you have to concentrate on what you are becoming!

Serve with Martha's Hand and Mary's Heart

As you begin to reach out and touch the lives of others, remember the importance of balancing the work of Martha's hands as she served, with the gift of Mary's heart as she sat and listened. A balance of both allows God to minister *through* us as we serve and *to* us as we listen.

These are some of the ways you can serve others with Martha's hands and Mary's heart:

Extend hospitality. "Be hospitable to one another" (1 Pet. 4:9).

Genuine hospitality involves opening your heart and your home, selflessly sharing what you have. Hospitality is reaching out to others in caring love and warmth. Whether it's inviting kids over after school, having the soccer team over for hot dogs, hosting a Bible study in your living room, or sharing with a neighbor over coffee—put that welcome mat out!

Nancy is the epitome of hospitality, one of the most giving people I know. There's always someone coming through her door! Everyone feels comfortable and welcome in her home. On any given day you can find three or four friends who have dropped by for advice or a quick visit. They may have 30 kids from Young Life (a ministry for teens) in their backyard on Saturday night, and 20 people in their family room for a Bible study the next Tuesday night. From weddings to receptions and parties (even my 40th "Gone with the Wind" birthday party), laughter and memories are a part of her household. Nancy is a gift to all who know her. She exudes the love of Christ to others.

Help those in need. "Serve Him with a whole heart and a willing mind" (1 Chron. 28:9).

Look around you. What can you do to help someone in your new community or church? What do you enjoy doing for others? Whatever touches your heart, find a need and fill it.

Joan keeps newborn babies in her home until they are adopted. She puts her life on hold to give her time and energy to infants who may be part of her life for only weeks or months. She also does volunteer work with inner city kids. She took a Spanish class in order to speak their language. Joan gives her time and her heart to children who need a mother's love. Her arms are an extension of Christ's love to those in need.

Give encouragement. "Therefore encourage one another and build up one another" (1 Thess. 5:11).

An act of kindness, a note of reassurance, a word of cheer, or a gesture of support are all forms of encouragement from one person to another.

My friend, Mary, is a consistent inspiration to the women in her life. At one time or another, everyone she knows has gotten an encouraging note, or has been on the receiving end of her kindness. She once sent a card to a friend each week for months during a very stressful time. When one couple was struggling financially, she had them come for dinner almost every week to encourage them. Her acts of kindness demonstrate sensitivity to the people in her life and their immediate needs. Mary reflects the love of Christ in everything she does.

Be of service to others. "But the greatest among you shall be your servant" (Matt. 23:11).

Be the first one to pitch in and do what's necessary in a time of need. Be someone who is dependable, organized, and who follows through on what needs to be done.

Sandy is the kind of friend everybody would love to have. When it comes to helping her friends, no job, task, or project is too big or too small. She helped a friend pack up her home and move for three days straight. She does unglamorous volunteer work once a week. She has cooked meals and cleaned house for friends when they are ill. Sandy has a willing heart and a loving attitude. She gives herself as a gift to others and demonstrates love by serving.

These are four women in my life who serve in different ways, but with the same heart. They serve not to bring attention to themselves, but to bring honor to Christ. What they do and who they are is an overflow of His presence in their lives. Whether being hospitable, helping those in need, giving encouragement, being of service to others, or ministering in countless other ways, we all must reach out and touch someone! How do we start?

- Be available. Your life is probably the least cluttered it will ever be after you move. Let people know you have free time and are available. They won't know if you don't tell them.
- Be aware. Put up your antennae! Look around. Be sensitive to what is going on in people's lives.
- Be approachable. Be warm and friendly even though it may be hard because you're new. People need to feel comfortable to approach you and start a conversation.
- Be accepting. Don't judge a person from the outside until you know them on the inside. There's always more there than meets the eye.

God will do incredible things in you and through you as you begin to move in the right direction and serve others. Just watch and see.

♥   Heart Talk   ♥

I want to give you a Garden Party! You've come this far, so today let's celebrate YOU—the person you are and the person you are becoming. I'll bring the flowers, you just show up! Wear a straw hat with a wide brim, and don't forget your Sunday dress. This is not an ordinary day! Pull up a wicker chair. The table is set with lemonade, fresh fruit, and scrumptious muffins. (Just for today, let's forget the fat content!) I've put out my grandmother's china with my best linen napkins and placed a rose across your plate.

In the middle of the table are flowers in a crystal vase. They are for you. They are the loveliest blooms from the garden—roses, Queen Anne's lace, and peonies. All around you are the colorful faces of zinnas, petunias, daisies, and poppies. The clay pots are filled with geraniums. Nothing is too good for you! You are worth it all.

Let me sit across from you as we sip our lemonade, and tell you how glad I am you came! (Whenever Bill and I went home for a visit, my daddy would always say over and over again, "Have I told you how glad I am you came?") We've become good friends through these chapters. You probably didn't realize we had so much in common. I really felt like I knew you all along. I look at you now and see how your life is just beginning to bloom. New beginnings have a way of doing that if we keep our faces to the sun. You'll make it because you have so much going for you! You've got me in your corner, and I'll be praying for you. You have a God who loves you and will never leave you. You've got a fresh start with each new day.

You'll notice behind you are helium balloons attached to the back of your chair with colorful ribbons. You have something in common with these balloons, believe it or not. You are both tightly held with limited boundaries. Suppose you reach back and untie them from your chair. What happens if you hold them loosely in your hand, then let go? As you look up and watch the balloons drift farther and farther away, lost in the magnitude of the sky, think about the things that you are tied to and watch them become smaller and smaller against the magnificence of God.

Now as you feel the warmth of the sunshine, also feel God's assurance of His peace and hope for tomorrow. You can now start over. Take your beautiful bouquet of flowers with you as a reminder that you are a fragrance of Christ to those around you. You can now look forward and move ahead.

Epilogue

The One Who
Moves with Me

*What lies behind us, and what lies before us, are tiny matters
compared to what lies within us.*
William Morrow

To understand the heart of this book, you have to go back with me to
1987. That's when it all started—the dream, the vision, the reality of
starting a ministry for newcomers. The three-step process of letting go,
starting over, and moving ahead that I worked through after my move
changed the course of my life and prepared my heart to begin a newcomer's
ministry. As I mentioned in chapter 1, if this process helped me through the
trauma and transition of moving, why couldn't it help other women going
through the same feelings and emotions? So began the dream.

Our church draws a lot of new people who move to our fast-growing
area. Although we offered once-a-month coffees to welcome the new
women who came, God nudged my heart with the question, *What's happening to these women after the coffees? Why don't we see them again?* I saw the
need for weekly contact and support, the need for nurturing and enfolding,

and the need for biblical teaching. It was critical for these women to process the feelings and emotions that accompany this change in their lives. So why not have a newcomer's support group and Bible study for these women? That's how my vision began.

My journey through the three stages became the basis for the class. In September 1987, after much prayer and encouragement from friends, I started the newcomer's ministry. The dream and the vision became a reality. Since then, God has used this ministry to help hundreds of women through the moving process. No matter where the women come from, and what their ages or backgrounds are, the concept has worked. The principles have held true semester after semester.

Other churches across the nation have since started newcomer's ministries. They recognize the impact the ministry has upon church growth by enfolding new women and their families.

The Apron Story

There are many wonderful stories of the effect this newcomer's ministry has had on countless women over the years. One particularly memorable story happened at an end of the semester luncheon given by the newcomers.

After everyone finished eating, the leadership team was asked to stand at the front of the room. Each woman from the class put on an apron that she had brought from home. Then the women brought out three new, matching, pink, handmade aprons and put one on each of the leaders. One of the newcomers took long pieces of pink ribbon and draped them over the sides of the leaders' apron sashes. She gave each leader a pair of scissors tied with a pink bow. Then the 20 newcomers came up, took the scissors, and cut a small piece of the ribbon from the sashes.

As each one cut a piece of the ribbon, she said, "We're cutting our apron strings. We're ready to move ahead with our lives now. You felt our pain as we let go, you showed us how to start over, and then you gently guided us to move ahead—always keeping God as our focus."

I still have my pair of scissors tied with the pink bow and I smile with fond remembrance every time I wear my apron.

A Turn of Events

As newcomer's classes ministered to women from semester to semester, people began to ask, "Have you thought about writing a book for newcomers? How about a manual for other churches to use in starting a newcomer's ministry?" I thought these were strange questions because writing a book or a manual was never in my wildest thoughts! My dream and vision for a ministry to newcomers in our church had become a reality. That was enough. I was happy teaching and loving those women, watching God change their lives in the process. Little did I know what God had planned.

The book talk continued, and God planted more seeds of encouragement, and then more, and more. And finally my heart began to have a new dream and a new vision. In July 1989, my life changed dramatically. My daddy, whom I adored, and still refer to as the last of the true southern gentlemen, died instantly of a massive heart attack in a grocery store.

Bill and I had told Mama and Daddy to wait in the front of the store while we went to get a few groceries. We were in the back of the store when I heard Mama scream. I dropped my groceries and ran through the checkout counter to get back to them. I had no idea how my life was going to change the minute I sped through that row of checkout counters.

Mama had not been in good health, and I thought something had happened to her. But not to Daddy, who had never been sick a day in his life. I have often said that at the moment of Daddy's death, I lost Mama, too. She never recovered emotionally from losing him.

I did not allow myself to grieve for Daddy. My primary thought was taking care of Mama and trying to get her through this. I spent the rest of the summer in Florida with her. It was one of the most emotionally painful times of my life. I watched her pain and grief, but didn't deal with my own until the next summer.

Passing the Baton

I came back to Phoenix in early September, just in time to start teaching another year of newcomers. By the spring of 1990, I let the spark of writing a book rekindle. God was opening too many doors and making it too obvious for me to deny that this was the next step in His plan—to take this ministry beyond our church walls.

The trips back and forth to Florida that year were hard on my teaching, and the thought of tackling a writing project led to only one conclusion: I would have to give up teaching newcomers.

I began to pray for the right person to teach and lead this ministry at our church. It was time to pass the baton. It had to be someone who loved Jesus

Christ, had a heart for new women, had walked in their shoes, had felt their pain, and had gone through the class. The right person was Darlene. She is a gift to me through her faithfulness to the ministry, and a gift to the many newcomers whom she continues to teach, nurture, and enfold at our church.

Between Then and Now

In September 1990, my brother called and said Mama had been diagnosed with lymphoma. I was on the next morning's flight to Atlanta. She was in the hospital from September to the end of October and I never once left her side. I watched the pain, the chemotherapy, the side effects, the needles, the hair loss and personality changes, the horror of the cancer spreading all over her body, and finally the deterioration of her mind. She died three months after her diagnosis, the day before my birthday. Those three months were physically and emotionally devastating for me. They seemed to follow so closely on the heels of the summer before, when Daddy had died. My grief was intensified by losing both my beloved Mama and Daddy within 16 months of each other.

When I returned to Phoenix after the funeral in November, I wasn't emotionally able to even think about writing a book. I stepped back from most of my commitments, realizing I had to deal with my own grief, feelings, and emotions. This time I couldn't bury my pain in busyness. I was sliding downhill fast and knew if I didn't do something, I would end up at the bottom.

In March 1991, four months after Mama's death, our family home of 35 years was sold. Once more, I flew back to help dismantle the house and pack, keep, or sell all our family possessions. I said good-bye to a town, a home, and old family friends. I then returned to Phoenix to continue putting all the pieces of my own life back together again.

In July 1991, our business began to go downhill during the hotel recession. Bill's only business project took him out of town for six weeks out of seven. Our marriage began to feel the strain of being apart, and our income dwindled. As things continued to get worse, we realized we had to make some drastic changes or we'd go under, both personally and professionally. In July 1992, we sold our house, sold our van, sold everything we didn't need, and rented a small patio home to cut expenses. I went to work full time. Bill pursued any and everything in the job market which enabled us to stay in Phoenix.

In July 1993, I got a phone call from John Trent, who has encouraged me and believed in this book project from the beginning. He said, "Are you going to the Christian Booksellers Convention?" I asked, "Where is it?" He replied, "Atlanta." Well, Atlanta was the very place I was going to be the week of the convention! *Timing,* I thought. *God's plan is in His timing, not mine, and it happened just when I am at my lowest about this book ever becoming a reality!* The encouragement I received at the convention renewed my hope in my capabilities, and I returned home, ready to write. When Bill picked me up from the airport, he saw that old spark in my eyes. It had been a long time coming. The first thing he said was, "You've got to quit work if you're going to give this 100 percent." So I stepped out in faith, quit work, and started writing and submitting book proposals all over again.

Today, one year later, the simple idea that started many years ago has become a reality! This book has been in process for four years. I couldn't have written it one day sooner than God had planned. I understand how all that I've been through during the last four years was part of my preparation to write this book. You see, I'm an ordinary person whom God asked to do an extraordinary thing. I had never planned to write a book. I had never planned to be talking to you like this, but I've learned never to underestimate an almighty God who wants something done. I am merely His vessel. I stand in awe on the sidelines as I watch Him work in my life and now in yours. He is the God who moves with me through every intricate part of my life. *Great is His Faithfulness!*

Appendix

Twenty Additional Tips from Women Who Have Moved

"Hang in there. Cry as much as you want, but not all the time in front of your kids. Make your needs known, but realize that it may be God who meets them and not your husband. Get a map. Look out the window. Explain to your kids what's going to happen. Pray and be honest with God. He can take it. Don't think of it as being lost, think of it as exploring. If you don't like the first doctor you go to, try another one. This goes for restaurants, grocery stores, dry cleaners and friends. Take a bath. Get a manicure. Cry. Laugh. Go to garage sales. Take yourself to lunch. Find things to be thankful for. Buy yourself flowers for the kitchen. Teach your kids how to cook."

Dianna H.

"Don't expect too much from yourself or your family. Everything is affected when you move. Realize you may be on an emotional roller-coaster, so develop your sense of humor! Don't try to anticipate what may happen tomorrow or next week. Just live in today."

Judy W.

"Trust God . . . even when it seems that everything is mixed up."

Julie M.

"Enjoy each day. Focus on being rather than doing. Admit the loss you feel, give it to the Lord, and move on."

Teri C.

"Don't withdraw into the four walls of your house. You will have to make the effort to fit into the community and you will have to 'make the first move' toward making friends. People won't come knocking at your door. Use this time for growth. Leave your comfort zone. Discover the woman God wants you to be."

Alma S.

"Have a family prayer time. Share all your feelings. God will provide all that will be important for your family. Don't worry about anything (house, etc.). Put everything into your family and everything else will come together."

Pam J.

"Reach out to others. There are plenty of people more needy than you are. Get close to the Lord; He is all you will have in the beginning."

Joan L.

"Don't fight it. Submit to God, He knows what is best for you. Submit to your husband; he wants what is best for you."

Marian G.

"Communicate daily with your spouse, and every few weeks ask each other, 'How are we doing?' Be honest with the Lord. It's okay. to cry and have 'rainy days.' Create a home that is a haven for your family, a joyful place of familiarity. Get out and get involved."

Debbie T.

"Be prepared to be an initiator in order to build relationships. Find a church home. Exercise. Volunteer. Find a good hairdresser."

Sudie A.

"Accept it. Don't fight it. Trust in the Lord and know that this move is part of His plan for your life."

Alma M.

"Please learn that your security comes from Christ alone. The move is unsettling. Time will heal. Allow yourself to grieve your loss and to feel lonely. Look at it as an opportunity to have a new start, new friends."

Robin A.

"Don't expect too much too soon. Pray about everything. Listen to your children's needs and support your husband. Get involved. Pace yourself in getting your house finished and realize 'Rome wasn't built in a day.'"

Beverly H.

"Try not to compare. Be patient. Reach out."

Joan M.

"Open your heart to a friend; she probably needs one too. Be patient; you won't click with everyone, but God will have someone special waiting."

Debby A.

"Work on projects that are incomplete. Ask a lot of questions. Exercise regularly. Believe and trust that God has good things in store for you. Dwell on the positive."

Gina A.

"Treat yourself to an ice-cream cone."

Betty M.

"Refer to your new residence as 'home' as soon as you move. I really think this helps a person let go of the past and move into the present."

Karen O.

"Stop and smell the flowers. Reach for the stars. Embrace life. Hold on to that which is most dear. Seize the day. Remember to say 'I love you.' Start a tradition. Enjoy the simple things. Don't complicate life. Bounce back. Redefine your life. Look at the big picture, not just the corner you're in. Laugh. Choose joy. Bake brownies. Put a bird feeder outside your window. Be flexible. Remember each day is a fresh start. Count your blessings. Put out a welcome mat. Say your prayers every night."

From my heart to yours,

Susan M.

Notes

Introduction
1. Kristin A. Hansen. *Geographical Mobility*: March 1991 to March 1992, U.S. Bureau of the Census, Current Population Reports, P20-473, U.S. Government Printing Office, Washington, D.C., 1993. 1.

Chapter Two
1. Miriam Neff. *Women and Their Emotions* (Chicago: Moody Press, 1983), 114-116.
2. Audrey T. McCollum. *The Trauma of Moving:Psychological Issues for Women* (Newbury Park, Calif.: Sage Publications, Inc., 1990), 71.

Chapter Three
1. Paul Tournier. *A Place for You* (New York: Harper & Row, 1968), 162-164.

Chapter Four
1. Kristin A. Hansen. *Geographical Mobility*: March 1991 to March 1992, U.S. Bureau of the Census, Current Population Reports, P20-473, U.S.Government Printing Office, Washington, D.C., 1993. 1.

Chapter Five
1. Elaine St.Johns. "A Member of the Family," *Guideposts*, July 1989, 21-22.

Chapter Eight
1. Sylvia Fair. *The Bedspread* (New York: Morrow Junior Books, 1982).

Chapter Nine
1. Gail MacDonald. *High Call, High Privilege* (Wheaton, Ill.: Tyndale House, 1986), 58-59.

Chapter Eleven
1. Vance Packard. *A Nation of Strangers* (New York: David McKay, Inc. 1972), 4-5.
2. Ben Ferguson. *God I've Got a Problem* (Ventura, Calif.: Regal Books, 1974), 43-44.
3. Tim Hansel. *Through the Wilderness of Loneliness* (Elgin, Ill.: David C. Cook, 1991), 29.

4. Elisabeth Elliot. *Loneliness* (Nashville: Oliver- Nelson Books, 1988), 158.

Chapter Twelve

1. For more information on Dr. Bill Yarger's tapes, "A Bibical View of You," write to Phoenix Seminary, 7601 East Shea Blvd., Scottsdale, AZ 85260.
2. Margery Williams. *The Velveteen Rabbit* (New York: Simon and Schuster, Inc., 1983), 5-6.

Chapter Fourteen

1. John Trent. *LifeMapping* (Colorado Springs, Colo.: Focus on the Family, 1994), 206.
2. Kristin A. Hansen. *Geographical Mobility*: March 1991 to March 1992, U.S. Bureau of the Census, Current Population Reports, P20-473, U.S.Government Printing Office, Washington D.C., 1993. l.
3. Susan Mernit quoting from Marilyn Segal in "Good-bye House," *Parents* Magazine, May 1990, 117.
4. Lawrence Kutner. "Parent & Child," *The New York Times*, January 18, 1990.
5. Susan Mernit. quoting from *American Association for Counseling and Development* in "Good-bye House," *Parents* Magazine, May 1990.
6. Donna Otto. *The Stay-at-Home Mom* (Eugene, Ore.: Harvest House, 1991), 127.
7. Source unknown.

Chapter Fifteen

1. Dee Brestin. *The Friendships of Women* (Wheaton,Ill.: Victor Books, 1988), 16.
2. Kathy Narramore and Alice Hill. *Kindred Spirits* (Grand Rapids: Zondervan, 1985), 28.
3. Jerry and Mary White. *Friends & Friendship* (Colorado Springs, Colo.: NavPress, 1982), 13.

Chapter Sixteen

1. Darien B. Cooper. *The Beauty of Beholding God* (Wheaton, Ill.: Victor Books, 1982), 11.
2. Tim Hansel. *You Gotta Keep Dancin'* (Elgin, Ill.: David C. Cook, 1985), .54-55.
3. Ibid., quoting Paul Sailhamer, 54.

Chapter Seventeen
1. Earl Wilson. *Self-Discipline* (Portland, Ore.: Multnomah Press, 1983), 6.
2. Dale Hanson Burke. "Making Those Dreams Come True," *Today's Christian Woman*, Sept./Oct. 1984, 42.
3. Charles L. Wallis. quoting Henry David Thoreau, in *The Treasure Chest* (New York: Harper & Row, 1965), 135.
4. Joseph Allison. *Setting Goals that Count* (Grand Rapids: Zondervan, 1985), 20-21.

Chapter Eighteen
1. Warren Wiersbe, quoting Oswald Chambers, in *With the Word* (Nashville, Tenn.: Oliver-Nelson Books., 1991), 362.
2. Jean Fleming. *Between Walden and the Whirlwind* (Colorado Springs, Colo.: NavPress, 1985), 64, 67.

The Newcomer's Ministry referred to in this book is an outreach ministry to women who are new to the community. It is designed to enfold, support and encourage these women. It provides a biblical group study that pertains to the adjustment and transition of moving. It enables new women to feel the care and love of Jesus Christ through others and encourages them to grow strong and deep in their relationship with Christ as they establish new roots. A leader's manual and workbook to accompany *After the Boxes Are Unpacked* is available through N.E.W. Ministries.

For more information on how to start a Newcomer's Ministry in your church, write to me at the following address:

> Susan Miller
> NEW Ministries
> P.O. Box 5692
> Scottsdale, Arizona 85261-5692

I would love to hear from you! Tell me your moving story and survival tips so I can share them with other moving friends in our Newcomer's Newsletter. If you have recently moved or if you are moving, and would like to be put on our mailing list, please let me know!

Focus on the Family

Focus on the Family

This complimentary magazine provides inspiring stories, thought-provoking articles and helpful information for families interested in traditional, biblical values. Each issue also includes a "Focus on the Family" radio broadcast schedule.

Parental Guidance

Close-ups and commentaries on the latest music, movies, television and advertisements directed toward young people. Parents, as well as youthleaders, teachers and pastors will benefit from this indispensable newsletter.

Clubhouse Jr.

Youngsters ages 4 to 8 will delight in the great games, creative crafts and super stories that full the colorful pages of *Clubhouse Jr.* Every article educates and entertains—all with an emphasis on biblical values.

Clubhouse

Here's a fun way to instull Christian principles in your children! With puzzels, easy-to-read stories and exciting activities, *Clubhouse* provides hours of character-building enjoyment for kids ages 8 to 12.

Brio

Designed especially for teen girls, *Brio* is packed with super stories, intriguing interviews and amusing articles on the topics they care about most—relationships, fitness, fashion and more—all from a Christian perspective.

Breakaway

With colorful graphics, hot topics and humor, this magazine for teen guys helps them keep their faith on course *and* gives the latest info on sports, music, celebrities . . . even girls. Best of all, this publication shows teens how they can put their Christian faith into practice and resist peer presure.

All magazines are published monthly except where otherwise noted.
For more information regarding these and other resources, please call
Focus on the Family at (719) 531-5181, or write to us at
Focus on the Family, Colorado Springs, CO 80995.

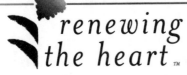

renewing the heart™

Focus on the Family's new collection for women

Focus on the Family's "Renewing the Heart" conference has encouraged, uplifted and provided renewal to thousands of women of all ages. And the "Renewing the Heart" selection of books will do the same! They feature sound, scriptural advice and teaching on topics that are relevant to today, like personal value and worth, security, ways to nurture and enhance relationships, and more. Best of all, they're from Focus on the Family. So you can be sure you'll be inspired, encouraged, and better equipped to handle the challenges you face . . . and uplift other women you know.

· · ·

Then God Created Woman

It's a simple fact: women are relational beings. Yet when it's intimacy we crave, we often turn to those who simply cannot fulfill our expectations. Realizing this, author and psychologist Deborah Evans takes readers back to the Garden of Eden to identify all women's deepest need—a close,intimate relationship with the Lord. For only when we wholly rely on God will we find freedom as the beautiful, confident creations He intended us to be: reflections of Himself. Paperback.

Kindred Hearts

All mothers and daughters share a deep, inner longing to be respected, cherished and adored *by one another.* And there's good news! Regardless of whether your present relationships couldn't be better or are less than ideal, you *can* fulfill that need. With keen insights and practical exercises, author Debra Evans helps women of all ages satisfy their yearnings for closeness with the people they're most intimately connected to—their mothers and daughters. Paperback.

Bless Your Socks Off

Encouragement has incredible power. Find out how to harness its benefits and add fulfillment and joy to your life with the step-by-step approach. Through humor, hope, and wonderfully crafted stories, popular speaker Sandra Aldrich provides inspiration and motivation to pass along a pat on the back and make someone's day—yours *and* the person's you bless! Paperback.

· · ·

FOCUS ON THE FAMILY®

Welcome to the Family!

Whether you received this book as a gift, borrowed it from a friend, or purchased it yourself, we're glad you read it! It's just one of the many helpful, insightful and encouraging resources produced by Focus on the Family.

In fact, that's what Focus on the Family is all about—providing inspiration, information and biblically based advice to people in all stages of life.

It began in 1977 with the vision of one man, Dr. James Dobson, a licensed psychologist and author of 16 best-selling books on marriage, parenting, and family. Alarmed by the societal, political, and economic pressures that were threatening the existence of the American family, Dr. Dobson founded Focus on the Family with one employee—an assistant— and a once-a-week radio broadcast, aired on only 36 stations.

Now an international organization, Focus on the Family is dedicated to preserving Judeo-Christian values and strengthening the family through more than 70 different ministries, including eight separate daily radio broadcasts; television public service announcements; 11 publications; and a steady series of books and award-winning films and videos for people of all ages and interests.

Recognizing the needs of, as well as the sacrifices and important contribution made by, such diverse groups as educators, physicians, attorneys, crisis pregnancy center staff and single parents, Focus on the Family offers specific outreaches to uphold and minister to these individuals, too. And it's all done for one purpose, and one purpose only: to encourage and strengthen individuals and families through the life-changing message of Jesus Christ.

• • •

For more information about the ministry, or if we can be of help to your family, simply write to Focus on the Family, Colorado Springs, CO 80995 or call 1-800-A-FAMILY (1-800-232-6459). Friends in Canada may write Focus on the Family, P.O. Box 9800, Stn. Terminal, Vancouver, B.C. V6B 4G3 or call 1-800-661-9800. Visit our Web site—www.family.org— to learn more about the ministry or to find out if there is a Focus on the Family office in your country.

We'd love to hear from you!